America's Most Haunted Encyclopedia Series | Vol. I

The Ghosts of Williamsburg, Richmond & Washington, D.C.

By US Ghost Adventures

T0204347

ISBN:
978-1-7355665-4-2 Paperback, Color edition.

Cover design by: In The Grey Design
Book design: Studio de Mel

Printed by Amazon on demand

First printed edition 2020

US Ghost Adventures Imprint
1006 Richmond Road, Suite 300, Williamsburg, VA 23185
www.usghostadventures.com

All photographs within are by US Ghost Adventures, with thanks to Terrence Riggins Photography and Chayna Sellers.

America's Most Haunted Encyclopedia Series | Vol. I

The Ghosts of Williamsburg, Richmond & Washington, D.C.

By US Ghost Adventures

America's Most Haunted Encyclopedia Series | Vol. I

The Ghosts of Williamsburg, Richmond & Washington, D.C.

By US Ghost Adventures

CONTENTS

CHAPTER I
The Ghosts of Williamsburg, Virginia   19

CHAPTER II
The Ghosts of Richmond, Virginia   59

CHAPTER III - PART 1
The Ghosts of Washington D.C.   **101**

CHAPTER III - PART 2
Haunted Georgetown   **127**

"Maybe all the people who say ghosts don't exist are just afraid to admit that they do."

– Michael Ende, The Neverending Story

For the tour guides who make everything possible,
our followers whose curious minds allow us to explore a
world that science has yet to reveal. Thank you for your
dedication, enthusiasm, and energy.
And thank you for the stories.

With respect and reverence to all those who have passed,
may they rest in peace and happiness.

Acknowledgements

This volume is one part of a larger encyclopedia series devoted to unveiling the most iconic haunted places across the US. The series is the result of countless hours of research. Most importantly, it is from talking to the people of the cities whose stories we tell here. Ghosts live among us in one form or fashion, and they form a part of the heritage and history of our cities. We are privileged to share the stories of some of our greatest cities here, with you.

To the team who made this book possible we extend our gratitude.
The hours of research, proofing and fact checking have elevated this from a collection of stories to a true encyclopedia of the best stories of hauntings and history.

To you, the reader, whose curiosity and quest for knowledge about the ghosts of your hometowns, and of towns far away sustains our enthusiasm for sharing these stories.

May you never stop wondering and wandering.

About US Ghost Adventures

The stories are the most important part of what we do. We're always looking for new stories from people have experienced things firsthand. Our professional tour guides bring these stories to life, and they are the first to build upon and improve them over time...and as they experience hauntings themselves. These collected stories are the ones that elicit the most gasps and prompt the largest collective intakes of breath. We don't claim this collection is exhaustive, but they are guar- anteed to be the best ghost stories from the cities we present.

We strive to make our stories entertaining, and informative, over the years we have found that real life is truly stranger than fiction, as Mark Twain said, 'fiction is bound by possibilities, truth is not.' We too have found that truth trumps everything, and research always turns up entertaining, and historically accurate stories.

With this comes the brutal honesty of history. While many stories contain violence and unpleasantries, we are committed to providing you with uncensored accounts of the events that transpired at each location. We often have requests from Universities or Corporate groups who take our tour to review our content beforehand. They often tell us to remove stories on the evils of slavery and atrocities suffered by countless innocents throughout the centuries, and we refuse to censor our stories or water them down. We strongly believe we have an obligation to society and history, and to honor those who have passed by recounting their stories honestly.

Our tours evolved over the years, but never as dramatically as in 2020. We had been exploring new ways to share our stories with a broader audience through content and distribution, and the shutdowns from covid-19 added an extra urgency to our efforts as all operations ceased.

We launched an app on a platform called Junket, which uses GPS triggers and immersive media to allow you to transform your phone into a tour guide, so you can take a range of experiences any time, any place, anywhere. These include all of our ghost tours, which can be enjoyed at the locations we talk about, or from the comfort of your own home.

We also launched a streaming and on-demand content platform, called Ghost- Flix. GhostFlix offers tours and other media in nearly all of our cities available both on-demand, which can be viewed anywhere, any time, and live streamed ghost tours. Live events are hosted by one of our guides as they walk you through the hallowed streets, visiting haunted locations and telling their stories. It's a great experience for single viewers and groups, which allows viewers to hear the stories and see the places, without traveling there!

Let's not forget our best friend, who can quickly become yours at home too: Lily. Lily, whose tagline is "host a ghost," is often described as a haunted or Halloween version of Elf on the Shelf, used as a way to scare and prank your friends, coworkers, housemates, or family. She's great hiding in a dresser, on a bookshelf, lying in wait in the refrigerator, on a toilet, or in a number of other creative places.

Lily is based on a real haunted doll we have in our possession. A tradition from the old countries, notably the Vikings, Lily is meant to ward off other malevolent forces. Lily's background is traced to the early 1600s, unearthing reports of occult practices, pagan rituals, and warding rights imported from Europe by the Dutch Colonists of Lower Manhattan. Handmade figurines like Lily were left out to frighten off local spirits and new world ghosts, an archaic custom dating back to the Vikings and the Romans. the doll was crafted to mimic the infamous Countess Elizabeth Bàthory, and in doing so, the tradition stated she contains part of the Countess' menace. Báthory was a noblewoman condemned in the 1600s for killing over 650 people, and is referred to as the 'Blood Countess' and 'Countess Dracula.'

Lily is a limited-edition doll reproduced alongside the original Lily. She's the best option to spice up the spirit of Halloween season in your home, and the perfect gift.

As our tours have gone nationwide, so has this series of books, the best of our stories in book form. From sea to shining sea, and from the lakes of the north, to the bays of the South, ghosts are where people are, and where there are good ghost stories, we are there.

You can find all of our tours and services at **usghostadventures.com**

Introduction

Welcome to the Williamsburg, Richmond & Washington, D.C. Volume I of America's Most Haunted. We have spent countless hours collecting and editing the very best stories from the cities presented in this volume, we also drew on our ghost tours and firsthand accounts in Williamsburg, Richmond, and Washing- ton, D.C. Together, the stories captured here present tales of lives frozen perpetu- ally in limbo, unable to move on and rest in peace, and they capture moments in time, periods of history and perhaps most impor- tantly, lessons for us all.

Virginia and D.C. are rich in American history, and its accompanying ghosts, from natives, to the Revolutionary and Civil Wars. We're excited to start this series by covering ghost stories in and around the U.S. Capital, Washington, D.C. But first, we begin with Williamsburg, Virginia, the colonial capital of the first British Colony, and only a few miles from the his- toric Jamestown settlement. The other volumes in this series will cover more than 20 other cities, and other rich historical regions throughout our United States. Collectively they provide an unrivalled survey of the hauntings of the United States of America. We hope you enjoy the stories we have collected, we enjoyed collecting them.

LILY

LILY - A Halloween Season Tradition

Handmade Halloween dolls like Lily were left out to frighten off pagan spirits and new world ghosts, an archaic custom dating back to the Vikings and the Romans.
The tradition of protection from ghosts during October returns with LILY - HOST A GHOST

Use Lily to ward off other ghosts and ghouls around Halloween. Put Lily on a porch, hang her on a door, put her on a shelf, or use her to scare friends, family, and children. Don't put Lily in a room where you sleep! Make Lily move around and appear in a different place for others to find each morning.

WHO IS LILY? READ HER STORY HERE

Historians have tracked Lily's background to the early 1600s, unearthing reports of occult practices, pagan rituals, and warding rights imported from Europe by the Dutch Colonists of Lower Manhattan. Handmade figurines like Lily were left out to frighten off local spirits and new world ghosts, an archaic custom dating back to the Vikings and the Romans. The conquers of foreign lands brought with them a piece of their folklore as protection. The original Lily was delivered to a paranormal research group from its owner, who stated: "I found her outside my door one morning, with a note that said to not put her by mirrors or in the same room I sleep in. I gave her a flashlight so she could drain the batteries, but instead she made my lights flicker at night. My cat would not go near her, and my dog would just stare. At times I would be woken up from a dead sleep smelling burnt toast, or sometimes a sweet fruity smell. Her favorite color is red. That is all I know."

Upon further research, the doll was crafted to mimic the infamous Elizabeth Bàthory, and in doing so, the tradition stated she contains part of the Countess' menace. Báthory was a noblewoman condemned in the 1600s for killing over 650 people, and is referred to as the 'Blood Countess' and 'Countess Dracula'.

LILY is a limited-edition doll reproduced alongside the original Lily. She's the best option to spice up the spirit of Halloween season in your home, and the perfect gift for any person or family, as she can both protect, and haunt! Bring Lily home and experience the supernatural first hand... If you dare!

usghostadventures.com/lily

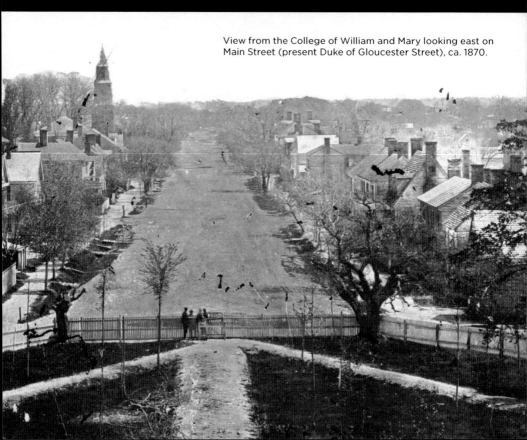

View from the College of William and Mary looking east on Main Street (present Duke of Gloucester Street), ca. 1870.

CHAPTER I

The Ghosts of Williamsburg, Virginia

If you see a rope flung out of the second story window of the Brafferton house of the College of William & Mary a small Native American boy may soon follow to run around the sunken garden. The ghost of an unwilling student at the second university in the colonies.

Such is the stretch of history in Williamsburg and that history lies heavy in these parts. Key in the struggles of the American revolution, Capital of the Colony of Virginia, site of the Battle of Williamsburg during the Civil War, alma mater of three American presidents, a slew of American firsts and to-day the leading tourist attraction in Virginia with Colonial Williamsburg a living, breathing connection to our past.

The ghosts of Williamsburg run thick and fast on this high ground between the York and James rivers, our stories here feature all the main periods from the storied history of this important town.

The Thomas Moore Story

Thomas Moore was a young man who was handsome and charming. He had inherited a house in Williamsburg from his older brother who had been killed in the Civil War. Thomas had a reputation as a flirt and a womanizer which meant that no one was surprised when he became involved in a three months-long fling with Constance Hall.

But Constance was married. Yet her husband was away on business, which gave the two lovers opportunity for their affair. They were often seen walking arm in arm. When Mr. Hall returned to town, he was told of the situation, and he did not hesitate to respond.

Mr. Hall burst into Thomas Moore's house and killed him on the spot. He then forced his wife to help him hide the body – dumping it in the basement of Moore's house. The couple was seen leaving the building by several witnesses. But it was not until Moore's disappearance that people became suspicious. The local authorities then went to visit the Moore House and discovered his savaged body in the basement.

Mr. Hall plead guilty to the crime, on condition that his wife would be let free. He was sent to prison and remained there for 8 years until his death. Constance fled Williamsburg in disgrace. As for Thomas Moore, he has continued his wom- anizing into the beyond. His ghostly form has been spotted wandering the streets of Williamsburg.

At the William & Mary Bookstore, the manager was spending the evening alone in her office. Much to her surprise, she heard someone in the bookstore even though she had locked the doors. She went out to investigate and found a tall, pale man standing at the far end of the room near the cash registers. She rushed back to her desk and called the police. When they arrived, she insisted all the doors were still locked which meant that the man must still be inside. But none of the cops could find a single trace.

At the Precious Gem Jewelry store, there was a similar story of Mr. Moore's antics. An employee, staying late, heard someone tapping on the window. The employee peered out over the counters and saw the clear image of a man with a thick mustache looking back at her through the window. Then, right in front of her, he began to fade and melted away into nothing.

The Bruton Parish Church

Bruton Parish Church served as the place of worship for Thomas Jefferson and George Washington and Martha Washington's great-grandfather once served as Reverend. Most colonials did not want to be buried in the church's cemetery; they preferred to be with their ancestors in a family plot, on their own land. However, in 1724 the local Baptist Preacher, Reverend Jones, complained about this because he had to travel far and wide to conduct funerals.

The Bruton Parish Church.

Reverend Jones had an almost perfect life. He was well liked by his church and he was married to the love of his life. But this all came crashing down when his wife became deathly ill. As she began to fade, he told her he would never love another woman, and he could not live without her. And then when his wife passed, Reverend Jones was forced to travel far from town to get his wife's gravestone.

The hauntings began right after his departure. There were many who saw Mrs. Jones wandering the church grounds, peaceful in death as she patiently waited for the return of her husband.

Despite his vows, he brought back a new wife! After that the ghost of Mrs. Jones was heard sobbing in the church grounds. Even worse, Reverend Jones left instructions to have his second wife buried between him and his first wife – separating him from her. To this day, people hear the quiet sobs of the reverend's first wife. Some say she is the reason an organ plays on its own after midnight.

But there is more to the building. The Battle of Williamsburg occurred on May 5, 1862. Along portions of the wall surrounding the church, there are still inden- tations from bullets fired during the battle. The church was used as a hospital that treated both Union and Confederate soldiers. The wound- ed were laid inside and in the graveyard. Their blood stained many of the graveyard's tablet stones. When the southern soldiers died most were put in a mass burial site that eventually contained around 100 Confederate soldiers.

Many have seen soldiers in Civil War uniforms roaming the grounds of Bruton Parish. Not long ago two security guards spotted a man with an elon- gated neck, dressed in black clothing that looked like a nineteenth century outfit. He moved in
an odd way and he had ruby red eyes. The guards watched him turn from the street and then go into the church cemetery. They went to the cemetery to look for the man, but when they heard a noise inside the church, they assumed he had broken in.

When they entered the church, they heard a strange thumping sound. Flutter – thump, flutter - thump. They could barely see in the darkness but when they shined their flashlights across the pews, they saw hymnals floating in the air and then slamming against the walls. The guards fled and returned to their patrol car. They decided this specter was an angry ghost as his elongat- ed neck was a sign of being hanged.

Market Square: The Williamsburg Baptist Church

Another building stood where Market Square is today during the Civil War. The structure that was here during the Civil War was the Williamsburg Baptist Church, a large white church with massive columns and grand steps, built in the Greek Revival style architecture. The church was one of 30 buildings used as a hospital after the Battle of Williamsburg on May 5, 1862.

The Civil War was longer and bloodier than most had anticipated. Many thought the war would last four months, not four years. The first major battle resulted in more dead than in all the previous wars fought by the U.S. Neither side was equipped to bury the many dead, or to treat the hundreds of wounded. It was not unusual for the dead and wounded soldiers to lie on the field of battle for a week before being buried or brought to a hospital. During this time, wild animals often tore at the flesh of the wounded.

The Williamsburg Baptist Church.

New ammunition called the Minni ball contributed to these higher casualties. When fired, the bullet flattened out and created massive wounds. If a soldier was shot in the head or stomach, he would eventually die. The surgeons wouldn't treat him, because he was not a priority.

If a soldier was shot in the extremities, the Minni ball would shatter the bone and shred tissue. Fortunately, the surgeons could treat this wound, but their only prescription was amputation. If an amputation was performed, the soldier would probably not receive anesthesia. Chloroform was available to only a few, meaning that he would be awake during the procedure. The average amputation took 12 minutes, as the surgeons would saw off an arm or leg and then mend the wound. There was a 77 percent chance of surviving the amputation. Yet for every surviving wounded soldier two more would die from disease and infection like gangrene. Surgeons didn't stop to wash their hands because the spread of infection was not understood at that time; doctors quickly moved on to next patient as they had many amputations to attend to.

The Union Army had 98 surgeons at the start of the war. By the end, they had grown to 12,000. In the 1850s, 50 percent of all doctors in the U.S. had no medical degree or medical license. This meant that thousands of volunteer surgeons, were learning on the job. Yet there were some who liked the bloodshed and carnage, and at Market Square was one of the worst. Referred to only as the Head Devil, this doctor was the head surgeon at the makeshift hospital at the Williamsburg Baptist Church. The infamous surgeon would amputate at any opportunity, often removing the healthy limbs of wounded soldiers. Minor injuries resulted in extensive, unnecessary surgery that killed two thirds of those treated. Survivors after the war tried to hunt him down, but they could not find him.

Market Square Tavern is still haunted by those men who died in the Head Devil's butcher's shop. Hotel guests have reported the sight of men in Civil War uniforms pawing, digging and gouging at the soil as they crawl about the ground. When the apparitions showed themselves on a clear night, guests have said they could see the figures were missing arms and legs – the Head Devil's victims spending eternity searching for their stolen limbs.

Baptist Church on left, next to powder horn. Courthouse on right.

Peyton Randolph House

Over two dozen people have died in or around the Peyton Randolph House since it was built in 1715, and many of them have remained to haunt the home. The Randolph House was featured by USA Today as one of the most haunted houses in the U.S. It was built in 1715 and purchased by Sir John Randolph, the only colonial Virginian to receive knighthood. He later purchased the eastern lot in 1724.

After his death, the home was willed to his son, Peyton Randolph. Peyton was one of the founding fathers and served as President of the First and Second Continental Congresses and was a cousin of Thomas Jefferson.

The Peyton Randolph House.

The house's troubles started with the outbreak of the Revolutionary War. The governor of Williamsburg, Lord Dunmore, declared that any slave that abandoned his owner and aided the British army would gain freedom at the end of the war. Some of the Randolph's slaves did so, including Mrs. Randolph's personal slave, Eve. When the war ended, these runaway slaves were returned to their owners, and Eve was treated harshly. She was then sold when Mrs. Randolph died, separating her from her son.

From that day on, the house appeared cursed. The earliest report was from a written account by the Marquis de Lafayette himself. In 1824, he went on a grand tour through the states to speak with veterans of the war. While in Williamsburg, he stayed at the Peyton Randolph's house. On October 1824, Lafayette wrote:

"I considered myself fortunate to lodge in the home of a great man, Peyton Randolph. Upon my arrival, as I entered through the foyer, I felt a hand on my shoulder. It nudged me as if intending to keep me from entering. I quickly turned, but found no one there. The nights were not restful as the sounds of voices kept me awake for most of my stay."

Many unfortunate events also happened at the house. A pair of men shot each other in a quarrel. In two separate incidents two children died from falls, and a Civil War veteran died mysteriously. More recently, in the 1960s, the house served as an overflow dorm for students of William & Mary. A young man felt a light tugging on his arm as he slept, and thought he was dreaming. That belief was dashed when the bed began to shake violently. Yet when he got up the room was empty. The student fled that night, even refusing to return for his belongings.

The next story is of a local security guard. When he found himself in the Peyton Randolph House's basement, the entire house filled with a loud, otherworldly roar. He tried to run, but some invisible presence gripped him by the ankles, anchoring him to the ground. The guard desperately radioed for help, and ten minutes later it arrived. The officers found the door wedged closed, and had to force it open, immediately releasing the original guard from his trap. The story has been used as a warning during guard training, about the things that guards can expect when dealing with the Randolph House.

In a more recent haunting a woman who lived there, often called security to report that she heard cries of children in the attached Peyton Randolph House. Shortly after she died in 2000, a fire alarm went off in that small section. No one had access which meant they were forced to break in through a window. When they got inside, they found white material all over the floor, and a fire extin- guisher in the middle of the room. The fire extinguisher material was not on the walls, was not covering other objects in the room, and it did not go into any other room. They did not see any footprints on top of the material to suggest that an intruder was inside. When they looked closely at the fire extinguisher and picked it up, they found a perfect round circle of clean, untouched floor underneath it. They never found the pin, but no one can explain how this fire extinguisher made its way to the middle of this house, expended all of its contents in a neat and clean pattern, while apparently remaining in a stationary position on the floor, and without any footprints!

Why is the Peyton Randolph House haunted? In the 1930s during a brief excavation of the area, two archaeologists working for Colonial Williamsburg wrote that there were two Native Americans buried on the eastern lot of the Randolph House, and that they should not be disturbed. One shallow dig in the property uncovered Native American pottery on the lot, although they did not dig deep enough — only about 8 inches — to discover more. In addition, the homes that occupied the area had constructed large basements, which would have destroyed many Native remains. The people who lived in these homes said they knew Native artifacts and graves were under and around their property. In fact, one woman had demanded that she be allowed to keep some of the "valuables" which included Native American pottery: "Mother was upset and called them up and said the artifacts belonged to her and she wanted them back. They told her that anything they dug up she could have."

In 1941, the National Park Service dug under the eastern side of the Randolph House to build the tunnel for the National Historic Parkway, disturbing the two documented Native American graves. And it is likely that there were many other Native Americans buried around the Randolph House. This is the best explanation for the early hauntings in the home, and for its strong paranormal activity that gives it the title of the most haunted house of Williamsburg.

The Peyton Randolph House.

Watch video interviews here:
williamsburgghosttour.com/video/

Governor's Palace

Williamsburg was once the capital of Virginia and the Governor's Palace was the epicenter of state politics. The last governor at the palace was Thomas Jefferson who hated the city of Williamsburg. The original building was destroyed in a 1781 fire – just two years after the building had been abandoned when the capital moved to Richmond. At the time of the fire, it was a makeshift hospital. More than a century later, along with many other colonial buildings, the Governor's Palace was restored in the 1930s. Unlike most of the other buildings, builders found over 150 skeletons during the restoration. The Governor's Palace had been a hospital during the Battle of Yorktown which means that the bodies were the remains of American soldiers.

The Governor's Palace.

Guests frequently witness a phantom candlelight wandering the upper floors, and they often smell flames from the 1781 fire.

Yet there is also an urban legend involving the Palace. A young couple who were attending classes at William & Mary decided to jump the wall that surrounded the palace and take a moonlit stroll through the newly restored hedge maze. The wall was tall which meant that the young man needed to help his girlfriend up and over the wall. She then jumped down to the opposite side. But as he was pulling himself up, he heard the girl scream – yet the sound was abruptly cut off and became a gruesome gurgling. When he reached the top of the wall, he saw the tall, gaunt figure of a man with a metal scythe. He had slit his girlfriend's throat and was already running into the maze. The man, apparently, was an escaped patient from the nearby Eastern State Asylum.

Of course, a story like that never goes away. Even today students try to jump the wall and wander the hedge maze at night. Many have said they felt as if they were not alone, or as if someone was following just behind them. Security officers are familiar with the story, and they do their best to discourage thrill seekers. One guard near the maze, heard heavy footsteps. He waited as the footsteps grew closer, assuming that he would soon be dealing with some students. Yet as he stood in the entrance, his flashlight held high, the footsteps continued to come closer – until they were right in front of him. Then without a pause, they contin- ued into the night behind him, and he experienced a sudden, intense feeling of cold as the maze's phantom had seemingly passed through him.

Wythe House

The house of George Wythe is the original structure built in 1755. It served as the temporary headquarters for George Washington when he planned his attack at the Battle of Yorktown. Wythe was also the first Virginia signer of the Declaration of Independence. Mr. Wythe became well known as one of the first law professors at the nation's first law school at William & Mary and he taught Thomas Jefferson in the early 1760s.

Yet George Wythe met an abysmal fate. He was poisoned by his grandnephew who wanted to get his inheritance early. Fortunately, the poison was not fast acting, and Wythe was able to disinherit his nephew before he died. Neverthe- less, his grandnephew was never found guilty, but, at the same time, he did not inherit the fortune he had killed for. And while this history fills the house with sorrow, it is another story that has caused the house to be haunted.

Wythe House.

One of the oldest legends in Williamsburg is that of the Lady Ann Skipwith. Along with her husband, the visiting Lady Ann was staying at this home. The wealthy couple attended an elite party at the Governor's Palace, but then Lady Skipwith began a bitter argument with her husband. Finally, she left and stormed out from the Palace. As she fumed and made her way back to the Wythe home, Lady Ann lost one of her red high heels. Back at the

Wythe House she found she had only a single shoe and one stocking covered foot. Still furious she stormed up to her room punctuated to the irregular snap of just one high heel hitting the wooden stairs. Three months later, Lady Ann Skipwith was dead – due to 'childbirth.'

A popular tradition among locals and William & Mary students is to summon the ghost of Ann Skipwith. They bring a red shoe to the door, knock three times, and declare, "Lady Ann Skipwith, Lady Ann Skipwith, Lady Ann Skipwith, we've found your red shoe!" Then, they hear the sound of her coming down the stairs with her signature clank-step sound.

One night, a group of college boys boldly walked up to the door, with a group of scared girls behind them. Vigilant security guards decided to frighten the students by rattling the door in front of them. The boys turned around and ran, knocking the girls down the steps; the girls followed immediately. But right after that, the security guards heard something themselves. They heard Ann walking down the stairs and later, they heard a woman singing happily in the house.

Employees said that they have arranged the furniture in a room, only to return a few minutes later to find the chairs and tables completely rearranged in a strange way. One evening during a special dinner held in the home, the sound of Ann on the stairs interrupted an otherwise uneventful dinner. One person went to check on what or who was making the footsteps and could find no one.

Others have seen the apparition of a woman, believed to be Ann Skipwith, walking through the house's backyard. Some guests at Williamsburg have seen the shutters open and close on their own. In addition, the apparition of a Revolu- tionary War soldier is often seen in the house.

While this story is told about the Wythe House, Lady Skipwith did not die in the house. Some now believe the haunting is, instead, the ghost of George Wythe's wife, who did die in the home. Some say that the sounds of footsteps are not   those of Ann Skipwith, but of Mrs. Wythe, who rushed down the stairs to confront her husband after he had returned from one of his late-night affairs.

Kimball Theater

Many feel that the most iconic image of the Civil War was that of brothers torn apart – countryman against countryman, brother against brother. In swing states near the Mason-Dixon Line, loyalties and opinions could be different enough that family members faced each other across the battlefield.

The Kimball Theatre.

The Ware Family's House stood where the Kimball Theater is now. When the Battle of Williamsburg tore through the city on May 5, 1862, furious combat took place in the streets. Residents who witnessed the battle saw bodies strewn about and heard the cries of men who were dying.

Outside the Ware House, one young Confederate soldier called out, begging for help. Mrs. Ware saw the soldier and helped him and others into the house.

Unfortunately, she was no doctor and the young man died soon after. Mrs. Ware covered him with a blanket and waited for the battle to end. When the battle was finally over and the Union swept through the city, Mrs. Ware's house served as one of 30 makeshift field hospitals.

A passing Union officer entered her house to see if his brother was there. When he stood above the soldier whom Mrs. Ware had helped, and pulled back the top of the blanket, he saw the face of his younger brother.

While both were native Virginians, one had joined the Confederacy, while the other had remained with the Union. And ultimately, neither would survive the war.

But the impact of seeing his brother dead on the table was enough to bind the elder brother to the location just as violent death bound the younger. Both have been seen wandering the halls of the Ware House that no longer exists, ignoring the different architecture and geometry of the Kimball Theater that took over the Ware House and altered it. It's as if the Ware House still stands, if only for those two brothers – one dressed in grey, and one in blue.

Employees have seen the brothers wandering through thin air, disappearing into walls and strangely playing with the faucets in the restrooms. People have witnessed the faucets turning on and off on their own.

Brafferton House

The College of William & Mary was founded by an English royal charter in 1693, making it the second oldest college in the U.S. after Harvard. It pre-dates Williamsburg as the capital of the Virginia colony. But long before 1693, Henricus, the second surviving English settlement after Jamestown, proposed building a college in 1619. However, the Indian massacre of 1622 killed about one-third of the colonials, and this college was never built. But when William & Mary was finally chartered in 1693, the charter contained a section that said the college would also provide a school for Native American boys. The purpose of the school was to train young men to become Christian ministers and to show them the virtues of English culture. When they returned to their tribes, they would serve as missionaries. It was hoped that this would help convert the Native Americans to the English way of life and prevent any further wars.

Brafferton House, the College of William & Mary.

However, this plan did not work well. The College could not get any Native vol- unteers for their school until 1707, when six boys were taken as prisoners by a warring tribe and given to the colony as tribute. This first class stayed with residents much like a foreign exchange program. Many students were abused and died of disease. And many of the boys did not speak the same Native language and fought with each other, as they were from different tribes. To create a better atmosphere for the students, a house was built for the boys in 1723. That house is the Brafferton House, also known as the

Indian School. The boys slept on the second and third floors, but they were still catching diseases from the colonists. This meant that many of them tried to escape to return to their tribes. In response, the college barred the doors preventing the boys from leaving. Consequently, many Native boys died inside the building.

Today students have come up the steps to sit, and then, from behind them, hear a doorknob turn. They might also hear the door shake, the sounds of voices behind the door, and hands pressing and scratching on the other side. It is believed that these are the ghosts of the young Natives who died in the building, unable to escape. A visiting professor who once stayed on the top floor of the building for a semester remarked that twice during his stay he was awakened in the middle of the night by the sounds of footsteps, voices, and a tom-tom drum beating.

The Brafferton house is home to the most famous ghost at William & Mary, a Native American boy who is still seen on campus. He had created a makeshift rope, threw it out the window from the second floor and climbed down to run around campus. Then he would return to the room to resume his studies the next day. One morning, a faculty member discovered the window open and a rope out the window. Next, they discovered that one of the students was unaccounted for. Soon they found his body in what is today called the Sunken Garden, the place where he was known to run. No reason was given for his death, but it is believed that a rival student killed him. Today, the boy is still seen running through campus, usually over the Sunken Garden.

The Sunken Garden

The Sunken Garden was built in the mid-1930s by President FDR's Civilian Conservation Corps and modeled after the Chelsea hospital gardens in England. The Sunken Garden is used for graduation ceremonies, concerts, classes, sports and special events. When the Native American boy from Brafferton House was alive, this is where he would run. But when he was alive, the garden was not sunken, as it is now, the surface was about 4 feet higher. Now, when his ghost is seen, he appears to be running above the Garden, up in the air where he ran when he was alive. He is wearing only a cloth skirt. Students have a tradition called the William & Mary triathlon that involves streaking through the Garden, in a manner like the boy's ghost.

The Sunken Garden, the College of William & Mary.

But there is more to the Sunken Garden. From 1775 to 1781, this area was known as The College Camp, where volunteers gathered to join the Virginia Regiment commanded by Colonel Patrick Henry, the same Patrick Henry who made the famous "give me liberty give me death" speech. The volunteers who met here left their homes and said their final goodbyes to their families, many for the last time, and then traveled north to reinforce General Washington's Northern Army.

Sometimes, a thick fog will slowly roll through, but will be confined to the Sunken Garden area. Within this fog, faint images of men are seen walking through the air where the military encampment had been located. People hear voices coming through the fog, rolling through the empty field, as the lights on either side of the Garden flicker, change colors, and dim out. This means that the Sunken Garden is host to both the ghost of the Native American boy and a revolu- tionary encampment.

36

College Camp Steam Tunnels

With the College Camp established during the American Revolution came underground tunnels used to store and hide supplies from the British. These underground tunnels were dug underneath the crypt in the College of William & Mary's Wren Building and were forgotten until the campus was expanded in the twentieth century. That was when tunnels were built to deliver steam heat to campus buildings. The steam tunnels incorporated parts of the old underground tunnels from the Revolutionary War and then stretched down through the Sunken Garden to buildings on both sides and across the street.

An entrance to the College Camp Steam Tunnels, the College of William & Mary.

The tunnels were easily accessible, as students could enter them through the Sunken Garden or from one of the many college buildings. This became a problem for three reasons. First, people who were homeless would use the tunnels for shelter. Second, crimes were being committed, including murder. And finally, fraternities and secret societies would force their pledges to enter the steam tunnels and enter the Wren Crypt, where they were told to steal a bone from one of the graves. In response, the College closed off most of the entrances and warned students that anyone caught in the steam tunnels would be automatically expelled.

The reason why the fraternities would make their pledges enter the steam tunnels was because the tunnels were haunted. Those inside would hear voices such as cursing, screaming, and sinister laughter. Yet once the students got

to the place where they heard the voices, there was no one there.
But they might feel as if someone was grabbing or breathing on them.
The steam tunnels are actually a

nice cobblestone walkway. One night when visitors were looking down into
one of the tunnels, there was about an inch of water. Then they saw distinct
disem- bodied footprints walk across the water making the impressions of a
shoe that appeared to walk across the surface.

The Ewell Building

Built in 1926, Ewell Hall housed the College of William & Mary's music department. It was original- ly named Phi Beta Kappa Hall, where the PBK's leadership and the campus theater were located. It also served as a women's dorm. When it was a dorm, an electrical fire destroyed much of the building, claiming the life of one girl. Her body was found near the front doors. She had tried to escape, but her exit was blocked by debris. John Rockefeller Jr. felt so bad about this disaster that he donated a quarter of a million dollars to repair the damage and build a new theater for the College down the street.

The Ewell Building, at the College of William & Mary.

Soon after the reconstruction, the music department moved into the north wing of the Ewell Building and students immediately noticed some strange happen- ings. Whenever the music room was left empty, people would return to find all the furniture in a different place.

Today, music teachers and students believe that the building is haunted. Many report that doors will open and slam on their own, and others see ghostly apparitions walking through Ewell's halls.

More frightening, students have reported that they can see the front doors shuddering at night. They say that it sounds like someone is trying to push the doors out, along with a frantic banging against the door. After the shak- ing dies down, a single woman's handprint appears on the window next to the door. People believe that it is put there by the ghost of the poor soul who was consumed by the Ewell Building fire and still seeks to escape.

The Wren Building

The Wren Building is an iconic building at the College of William & Mary. Named after the famous architect, Sir Christopher Wren, (and believed to be the building's designer), it was built between 1695 and 1700 and is the oldest academic building still in use in the United States. The students learned, slept and ate here. The Wren has a long and turbulent history. It was first destroyed by fire in 1705 and rebuilt with funds from Queen Anne, financed by money from pirates in 1716. During the Revolutionary War, it was used as a hospital for French soldiers wounded while fighting at the Battle of Yorktown in 1781. Behind the archway is a plaque which lists the names of more than 120 French soldiers who died while being treated for their wounds.

People have reported seeing a man in a French uniform wandering the halls at night – a bloody bandage wrapped about his head. He never stays for long and never acknowledges anyone. After a few seconds, he simply fades from view.

The Wren Building at the College of William & Mary.

In 1859, the Wren was destroyed by fire again and was rebuilt that same year. When Virginia seceded from the Union at the beginning of the Civil War, the College closed and the president and all faculty members, as well as most students joined the Confederate Army. Also, the College used its endowment to buy Confederate bonds which were worthless by the end of the war. The Wren was used as a Confederate barracks, and later as a hospital for the wounded.

After the Battle of Williamsburg, the Union Army occupied the Wren and used it as a hospital. Surrounding the Wren and in the College Yard were rows of wounded soldiers, as the Wren was overcrowded. Surgeons performed amputa- tions in the yard, as piles of amputated limbs piled up and the screams of soldiers filled the college grounds. The limbs that had been removed were tossed un- ceremoniously into piles that grew as high as a man is tall. Today, classes in the building have been stopped because of ghostly screaming that sometimes echoes through the building, a paranormal memory of these soldiers' pain.

William & Mary was on the frontlines of the Civil War, and as a result Williams- burg was under martial law. In September of 1862, following a Confederate cavalry raid through the college campus that killed 11 Union soldiers, members of the Union Army retaliated by burning down the Wren. During the Battle of Williamsburg, Union soldiers broke into the crypt, and took anything of value. This included prying silver ornamentation from the coffins. Such actions are known to anger the dead, and sudden cold tempera- tures are often felt in the vicinity of the crypt.

The Wren was rebuilt in 1868, and then remodeled to recreate its colonial look in 1929. The Wren Building boasts a couple of little-known secrets. The first secret is about one of the few locations not damaged by these fires, resting beneath the building's chapel, i.e., the Wren crypt. Many notable Virginians were laid to rest there, including the body of Sir John Randolph, his sons Peyton and John and Lord Botetourt. The second secret is that bullet holes are visible in the lower part of the building from the Civil War.

The President's House

This building has one of the best-preserved original exteriors in all of Williams- burg with more than a handful of resident specters. All but one of William & Mary presidents have lived in this house, but many U.S. presidents have stayed here as well.

The President's House at the College of William & Mary.

The house is the third oldest building on Old Campus and was built in 1733. And while it looks like the Brafferton across the way, it is four feet larger. On June 25, 1781, British General Cornwallis kicked out College President Madison, second cousin to the later U.S. President Madison, and used this home as his personal headquarters for ten days when his army stopped in Williamsburg before continuing to their resupply point in Yorktown.

After the British left, the pursuing French Army used the College grounds and home as a hospital. This house was a hospital for French Officers wounded at the Battle of Yorktown. On December 22, the French were still caring for wounded men and accidentally started a fire that destroyed the home's interior. It wasn't until five years later that a payment from Louis the XVI restored the building. In 1931, the house was restored to the colonial appearance of today.

Some of the visitors to the house have smelled the scent of smoke and fire, just before seeing the apparition of a smoldering man in French uniform crawling

on the ground, searching for an escape from the house. When approached, the phantasm will vanish, but his sounds continue through the halls. Former college presidents have remarked that they have heard footsteps walking on the stairs and in other unoccupied areas late at night. Doors and objects have been known to move on their own, and sometimes observers from the outside have spotted strange activity as well, such as seeing a French soldier peering out through one of the windows.

One president and his family who lived here had a problem. A closet door in one of the children's rooms kept opening and slamming shut on its own, especially in the middle of the night. The president called maintenance to repair the door, but when they arrived, they could not determine the problem, and they were unable to fix it. Yet no matter what was done to the closet door, it would refuse to stay closed. Even placing heavy furniture in front of it did nothing. Every morning, the door would be found open. Finally, they removed the door entirely, but this was the worst solution, as it brought about persistent rattling and banging on the floor below.

The source of the problem was finally discovered during building renovations. An electrician was working inside the building's crawlspace when he made a grisly discovery. It was a strange object that turned out to be a shard of bone sticking out from the brick that made up the closet. This brought investigators, both law enforcement and historical. They ultimately found the entire skeleton of a young girl somewhere between the ages of 12 and 13 within the bricks of the closet. The skeleton was removed and given a proper burial. Many said that after the skeleton was removed and buried the hauntings stopped. But that's not true. Objects still move on their own, and footsteps and strange sounds are still heard in the home.

Public Hospital

Few municipal buildings can evoke fear and revulsion like the mention of a mental asylum from the days before modern psychology. The type of "treatment" that took place was rarely helpful, and often cruel.

The Public Hospital for Insane and Disordered Minds was one of the first dedicated structures for treating the mentally ill in the United States. Although custom built for its purpose, the hospital was not built for comfort; patients would be chained to the ground behind heavy doors and given only straw for bedding with no heat to keep them warm. Built in 1772 and opened in 1773, the Public Hospital's mission was to benefit "persons who are so unhappy as to be deprived of their reason."

The Public Hospital.

Up to this point, the mentally ill were kept in the Public Gaol (British variant of Jail) and treated as prisoners. Yet the Public Hospital kept its patients in the same the conditions in the hospital were similar. The structure had 24 cells, designed to isolate each person, reinforced with a heavy door and barred windows. In 1799, two dun- geon-like cells were added for the wild, violent, and extremely insane. Ten-foot fences were erected at the perimeter to prevent escape when the patients went outside.

During the eighteenth century and much of the nineteenth century, mental illness was often seen as a choice. Early attempts to cure mental disorders included cold water immersion and blistering salves that would chemically burn the patient's skin. Patients would be dunked in cold water while their hands and legs were tied, or they would be zapped by electricity. They could also be cut and drained of blood in the hopes that the disease was in their blood.

Over time, the technology "improved" to include electroshock therapy and potentially dangerous pharmaceuticals. It was not until 1841 when Dr. John Galt arrived and became the hospital's superintendent that things began to change. Dr. Galt was a young forward-thinking man when he was chosen to head the Public Hospital. Each patient was given their own bed, recreation time and medicinal laudanum if their condition allowed. Improvements were almost immediate and the campus quickly expanded to seven buildings and 300 patients.

Unfortunately, the golden age was not to last. With the onset of the Civil War precious materials were diverted away from the hospital and towards the front lines. As a result, Dr. Galt harassed the local Union quartermaster for more supplies. He apparently became such a thorn in the side of the Union Army that he was banned from the hospital. Not long after, Dr. Galt overdosed on laudanum, which in turn led to a violent seizure. He was found face down on the floor of his house, across the street from the hospital, with a pool of blood beneath his head.

Many people have lived in the house since, and all have had to deal with the stained wood on the floors. One family even replaced the floor entirely, only to have the stain reappear on the new flooring. Many of them also saw the figure of a man, just like descriptions of Dr. Galt, wandering aimlessly through the halls.

The original hospital building was destroyed by an electrical fire in 1885, in which one unknown female patient was burned alive, and a second, Mrs. Jeffries, escaped only to drown in the James River several miles away. The female patient who was burned in the hospital remains to haunt it. One employee said, "Tour-   ists complain about sudden gusts of wind sweeping through the halls. What's even more strange is sometimes when we arrive in the mornings the bed in the exhibition room looks like it's been slept in... It's an odd feeling knowing someone is watching."

As for the hospital itself, the screaming of the tortured, insane patients can still be heard, muffled, as if heard through thick cotton. The lights often flicker and die, and gusts of wind rip through the museum despite the doors and windows being closed. More than 100 patients died while committed here. Their presence has been heard, felt, and seen in the reconstructed Public Hospital.

The Courthouse: Witchcraft

The Courthouse building was constructed in 1771 and served as a location for two separate court systems, that of James County and Williamsburg City. This court heard civil cases and petty crimes, not serious cases. The Declaration of Independence was also read aloud here in 1776. During the Civil War, the Courthouse was used as a hospital and morgue for Confederate soldiers following the Battle of Williamsburg in 1862.

But long before the establishment of this formal court in 1771, the legal system was flawed and was based on religion, faulty logic, and superstition.

The English settlers firmly believed that the Devil was in Virginia, especially after meeting the Native Americans. The Native's main spirit of worship was the god Okee, who the Virginia colonists saw as the Devil.

Here is what some prominent men of the time had to say:
-- Puritan minister, William Crashaw claimed that, "Satan visibly and palpably reigns in Virginia, more than in any other known place in the world."
-- Rev. Alexander Whitaker said the Indians were, "...very familiar with the Devil."
-- Original settler, George Percy, claimed that the Native Americans were, "...making noise like wolves or Devils."
-- John Smith even said the Chief Powhatan was, "...more like a Devil than a man."

Drawings of him led to this conclusion. With five-foot long hair and short on one side, his "ugly" appearance looked nothing like the Christian God. Therefore, with such talk of the Devil in Virginia, witchcraft came into play.

And it appears the average colonial citizen had to walk on eggshells to avoid being accused of witchcraft.

Here were some reasons for being accused:
- Being female
- A lot of female friends
- Too poor
- Too rich
- Argue with anyone
- Too old
- Too young
- Too many kids/Too few kids/No kids

- Strange or stubborn behavior
- Mole or birthmark
- Spoiled milk or butter in your home
- Unmarried
- Daydreaming about a future husband (aka predicting)
- Breaking Bible rules
- Having braids
- Being raped

The concept of witchery began before the colonists landed in the New World. They brought their beliefs with them from England. When they met the Native Americans, they felt evil was among them. In 1622, the colonists started accusing each other of witchery. Evidence shows around two dozen witch trials took place in Virgin- ia, but during the Civil War most of the trial documents were burned.

The case of Grace Sherwood is the most famous in Virginia. She was accused in 1698 and was put on trial in 1706 at the General Court, which looked similar to the Courthouse structure:
-- A townsperson said that Grace, "...bewitched our pigs to death and be- witched our cotton."
-- A neighbor declared, "Grace came to me one night and rode me and went out of the keyhole or crack of the door like a black cat."

Statements such as these could lead to a torturous trial and a test. Her hands and feet were bound and then she was thrown in the water. This was known as the "Water Test." If she floated, she was guilty; if she sank, then she was innocent because water is a pure element and it accepted her. But Grace floated, which meant that she was convicted and imprisoned. Then for 16 years she was tor- mented. Luckily, Grace was released by 1714 and the last witch trial in Virginia took place in 1730.

An older man who worked in Williamsburg for many years said, "Sometimes I will cut behind the courthouse back yard to get to my car at the end of a long day. I'd say two or three times, when I crossed the field, I heard a girl's faint voice so close to my ear saying, 'I didn't do it.' I do wonder if it's that Miss Sherwood." We cannot be sure if this is the voice of Grace or is, per- haps, the voice of another woman accused of witchcraft.

The Ludwell-Paradise House

The Ludwell-Paradise House dates to at least 1755 and was built in the Georgian architecture style. However, it is famous for the ghost of Lucy Ludwell, known as one of the most eccentric women in Colonial Williamsburg. Some called her crazy and she was the subject of conversation among the upper class in England and Williamsburg due to her energetic and mischievous personality. Lucy spent most of her life in London where she once threw a tea urn of boiling water on two men who had annoyed her.

Lucy was born in Williamsburg and she returned there in 1805, ten years after her husband passed away, and was allowed to live in the Ludwell-Paradise house although the Williamsburg property that Lucy inherited from her family was confiscated during the Revolutionary war because her husband was a loyalist who had supported England.

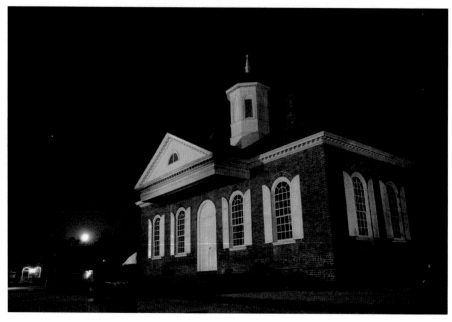

The Ludwell-Paradise House.

It was here that Lucy spent the remainder of her days, where she considered herself superior to the other residents due to her position in London. She was also obsessive and impulsive. When young James Monroe came to Williamsburg years before he became president, Lucy ran up to him and declared, "Sir, we have determined to make you President." Lucy was also known for borrowing her friends' clothes, especially hats.

Mad Lucy is best known for her unusual carriage rides. She had a carriage assembled in her back yard where she would invite visitors and callers inside. Then she would have a servant move the carriage back and forth to simulate a carriage ride to an imaginary destination. Lucy's carriage rides became frequent and she had trouble differentiating reality from fantasy.

In 1812, Lucy was committed to the asylum at Eastern State Hospital. Mad Lucy died in 1814, but many believe that her estranged spirit remains in the home. Lucy was a clean freak and took many baths each day. Many say they still hear the sounds of someone bathing upstairs.

Palmer House

In the late 1740's, John Palmer, a wealthy lawyer and a money handler for the College of William & Mary, moved into the home closest to the Capitol Building. One night in 1754, the Palmers awoke to a house filled with smoke, their fine home in flames! After the fire, Mr. Palmer replaced his burned-out dwelling with the structure that stands on the property today.

The Palmer House.

By the 1860s, the house was owned by Mr. Vest, a local merchant, who happened to be the richest man in town. Knowing that Williamsburg was vulnerable to attack, the Vests abandoned their property. After that the home became headquarters for Confederate generals who later abandoned the home before the Battle of Williamsburg. The Palmer House then served numerous Federal provost marshals assigned to watch over the city.

One night in 1865, a well-liked Union officer, Lieutenant Disoway, reprimanded a drunk soldier who had abandoned his post. Outside this house, the soldier grabbed a guard's pistol and shot Lieutenant Disoway.

Dr. Garret rushed from his home across the way to tend to the Lieutenant, but he could do nothing to save him. Lieutenant Disoway died within two hours of the shooting. Yet Disoway seems to have liked the house and the people, and his spirit remains in the Palmer House. Near the turn of the century, a family named Tucker lived in the residence.

Mrs. Tucker wrote in her journal entry dated June 23, 1896:
"We have become aware of a ghostly presence lurking within our home.
Late last evening, I was having trouble sleeping, so I went for some water.
As I rounded the corner of the parlor, I saw the transparent figure of a man
sitting in a chair! He had a pipe in his mouth and appeared to be dressed in
dark clothing with   gold trim. He sat crossed legged reading a book. My
fear overcame me, and I fell   to the floor. When I awoke the next morning,
I ran to my neighbor, Harriet, to   tell her of my experience. She suggested
that I research the house to learn of its past. She believes a spirit has made
himself comfortable in our home...In the archives of The College of William
& Mary, I found the story and picture of a   man who passed away years earlier in the house. I was shocked to find the man in the picture and the ghost
in my parlor, to be one in the same! I learned his   name to be Disoway. I am
hoping his spirit will pass on soon. We are frightened by him and fear what
he might do."

Secretary's Office and Jones Cemetery

Known as the oldest archive building in North America, the Secretary's Office was built in 1748. It was constructed in response to the Capitol Building fire that destroyed most of the public documents. The Secretary's Office was made of brick, the floor of stone, and there was to be no attic or base- ment. The two fireplaces kept the building warm and the documents dry and mold free. It was a very expensive building for its time.

The Secretary's Office.

The purpose of the property changed over the years especially when the capital moved to Richmond. In 1784 this building became a grammar school. Just a few years later it was turned into a rental property.

The structure is well designed and served as cover for a group of Confeder- ate soldiers during the Battle of Williamsburg. Marks made by rifle bullets, Minni Balls, can be found throughout the structure. These are bullet marks from the withering crossfire that the Union fired to flush out Confederates. Ultimately, the Confederates were cut down as the Union surrounded them. Rumor has it that on cold, crisp nights you can still hear the panicked shouts of the soldiers looking to escape.

In the cemetery next door, the most frequently seen spirit is that of Edna Jones. She lived in what had been the Secretary's Office in the early 1900s.

Having been converted into a house, the office now housed the enigmatic Jones family. David Roland Jones kept his many daughters locked away, and they were only seen once a week, at church. None the less, Edna caught the eye of a local food delivery boy John Mince, and the two made a promise to meet later that night at the former Governor's Palace grounds.

Edna was elated and prepared for her secret date. She put on her finest clothes, fixed her long, red hair and cleaned her thick eyeglasses before she set out just after dark to find the food delivery boy. Unfortunately, in the dark she was struck and killed by a carriage. Later she was buried outside the house that had been like a prison and joined in death by each sister in turn. The entire family is now buried there.

Security officers have seen a girl with long, red hair and thick glasses sitting in front of the window of the Secretary's Office, perhaps hoping to catch a glimpse of her secret beau. She will even be seen hovering over the graveyard – keeping watch over her family's plot.

Public Gaol

Few places evoke the type of human misery that one finds at a prison.
Little regard is given to those that have committed crimes, particularly back
during the colonial era – and the Public Gaol in Williamsburg was no
different. It was never designed to hold anyone for long; the Public Gaol was
a simply a location to place the accused until they were found innocent or
sentenced to branding, whipping or even execution. The floors were bare
stone covered in straw, and both disease and rats ran rampant through the
cells.

The Public Gaol.

When Williamsburg became the capital of the Colony of Virginia in 1699,
city officials realized that with economic growth came crime. They reached
out to the best building contractor in the state, Henry Cary, and authorized
him to construct "a strong sweet prison" in 1701.

At its inception, then, the Public Gaol only had three rooms: two for inmates,
and one for the gaoler. The jail held its first 2 prisoners in 1704 and served
as a jail until its closure in 1910. A "Debtor's Prison" was added in 1711, and
then a separate brick dwelling for the gaoler in 1722. But officials soon realized that this was not big enough; a thirty by twenty-foot building could not
support all the runaway slaves, thieves, Tories, and spies.

Unfortunately, despite all these additions, the Public Gaol failed to live up to
its "strong and sweet" expectations. The food was terrible (soggy peas and
overly salted beef); the cells were freezing, and many inmates died as a result.

In addition, "Gaol fever," or typhus, plagued prisoners and jailers alike.

Several high-profile prisoners spent time in the Williamsburg Public Gaol, such as Henry "Hair Buyer" Hamilton, a British official who hired Native American raiding parties to murder rebellious colonists, including women and children. Although he denied it, it was rumored that he paid a ransom for a colonist's scalp. Eventually, he was sent back to England as a prisoner of war.

The most notorious group to be imprisoned was Blackbeard's Pirates. Sixteen of Blackbeard's men that survived the final battle in 1719 were brought back to Williamsburg to await trial. In March 1719, 14 of these men were hanged in metal gibbets, or cages, along what would be known as 'Gallows Road,' which is today named Capital Landing Road. On the day of their execution they were carried from the Public Gaol to the gallows in a horse-drawn cart. They were brought before the executioner and hanged, one after another, until all 14 were dead. Their bodies were left to rot in the gibbets, a sign to all who passed through Williamsburg of the fate that befalls pirates.

However, most occupants of the Gaol were men and women awaiting trial in the General Court and the Court of Oyer and Terminer, or convicts awaiting brand- ing, whipping, or execution by hanging. First offenders would typically receive mercy by the court, and some offenders were simply fined. In any scenario, the Gaol was not designed for long-term imprisonment.

The jail also had a female population, and the ghosts of two women believed to   be family members of one of the jailers, are rumored to still lurk in the goaler's upstairs quarters. Security has reported hearing more than just the occasional footsteps. When employees walk upstairs to see what the noises were, they would find furniture turned on its side or props lying on the floor, across the room from where they were originally placed. The women's animated conversations and the thumping of their heavy shoes are also heard coming from the deserted room.

The Public Gaol is thought to be the second most haunted place in Williamsburg. Many people at night have heard the otherworldly rattle of the chains, their spirits forever searching in vain for some position of comfort on the cold stone floors. Stooped figures are seen, cowering in the far corner of their cells. Well known to security guards is a ghost that they call "Mr. Scratch," known to answer simply questions with one scratch for yes, two for no. When asked if he had known Blackbeard, Mr. Scratch said "Yes."

JOIN US FOR A GHOST TOUR!
USGHOSTADVENTURES.COM

Las Vegas, NV
Gettysburg, PA
New York, NY   Denver, CO   Asheville, NC   Myrtle Beach, SC
Salem, MA   Chicago, IL   Williamsburg, VA   Orlando, FL
Savannah, GA   Nashville, TN   Washington, DC   Honolulu, HI
Charleston, SC   Gatlinburg, TN   Atlanta, GA   Tampa, FL
St. Augustine, Fl   San Diego, CA   Richmond, VA   Dallas, TX
Key West, FL   Los Angeles, CA   St Louis, MO   Cincinnati, OH
New Orleans, LA   San Francisco, CA   Philadelphia, PA   Baltimore, MD
San Antonio, TX   Portland, OR   Charlotte, NC   Salt Lake City, UT
Austin, TX   Seattle, WA   Aspen, CO   Virginia Beach, VA
                         Miami, Fl   Phoenix, AZ   Nantucket, MA

CHOOSE YOUR GHOST ADVENTURE ON-SITE OR ONLINE

SELECT A PRIVATE GROUP TOUR IN A CITY NEAR YOU OR JOIN ONE OF OUR EXPERIENCED TOUR GUIDES LIVE-STREAM FROM ANYWHERE.

ATLANTA GHOSTS
ATLANTA, GA

Austin GHOSTS
AUSTIN, TX

BOSTON GHOSTS
BOSTON, MA

CHARLESTON TERRORS
CHARLESTON, SC

QUEEN CITY GHOSTS
CHARLETTE, SC

WINDY CITY GHOSTS
CHICAGO, IL

DALLAS TERRORS
DALLAS, TX

DENVER TERRORS
DENVER, CO

GATLINBURG HAUNTS
GATLINBURG, TN

CIVIL WAR GHOSTS
GETTYSBURG, PA

SOUTHERNMOST GHOSTS
KEY WEST, FL

LA GHOSTS
LAS ANGELES, CA

LAS VEGAS GHOSTS
LAS VEGAS, NV

MIAMI HAUNTS
MIAMI, FL

NASHVILLE GHOSTS
NASHVILLE, TN

NEW ORLEANS GHOSTS
NEW ORLEANS, LA

NYC GHOSTS
NEW YORK, NY

ORLANDO HAUNTS
ORLANDO, FL

PHILLY GHOSTS
PHILADELPHIA, PA

PHOENIX GHOSTS
PHOENIX, AZ

PORTLAND GHOSTS
PORTLAND, OR

RICHMOND GHOSTS
RICHMOND, VA

SALEM GHOSTS
SALEM, MA

RIVER CITY GHOSTS
SAN ANTONIO, TX

SAN DIEGO GHOSTS
SAN DIEGO, CA

SAN FRANCISCO GHOSTS
SAN FRANCISCO, CA

SAVANNAH TERRORS
SAVANNAH, GA

SEATTLE TERRORS
SEATTLE, WA

DC GHOSTS
WASHINGTON, DC

COLONIAL GHOSTS
WILLIAMSBURG, VA

OLD CITY GHOSTS
ST. AUGUSTINE , FL

St. LOUIS GHOSTS
ST. LOUIS, MO

NEPTUNE GHOSTS
VIRGINIA BEACH, VA

FEATURED IN

USA TODAY

(((SiriusXM)))
SATELLITE RADIO

HUFFPOST

CountryLiving

Inc.

Trvl CHANNEL

CBS

MTV

INSIDE EDITION

USGHOSTADVENTURES.COM

US GHOST ADVENTURES

Broad Street, 1905.

CHAPTER II

The Ghosts of Richmond, Virginia

Richmond is one of the oldest cities in the South. The fertile and beautiful lands occupied by Powhatan tribes reluctantly gave way to British settlers. A hub of early industry with plentiful energy from the James River, the downtown neighborhood of Shockoe Bottom was at the center of Richmond's slave trade. Between the late seventeenth century and the end of the Civil War in 1865, the area was the second largest slave trading center in the country, behind New Orleans.

Profits from the slave trade fueled the creation of wealth for Southern whites and drove the economy in Richmond, leading 15th Street to be known as Wall Street of the South in the antebellum period, with the surrounding blocks home to more than 69 slave dealers and auction houses.

This trade in human souls led to Richmond gaining wealth and power, becoming a powerful seat of government for the Commonwealth of Virginia. Richmond was also the capital of the Confederacy during the Civil War, until Union General Ulysses S. Grant forced Confederate General Robert E. Lee to evacuate the city, leaving a trail of fire, death and destruction in his wake.

The city recovered swiftly and entered the twentieth century with an advanced electric trolley car service and a prospering legal and governmental industry, as well as the first triple railroad crossing in the country. Antebellum life flourished for the free slaves in some quarters. In 1903 African American businesswoman and financier Maggie L. Walker chartered St. Luke Penny Savings Bank and served as its first president. She was the first female bank president in the United States.

In Richmond there are tunnels with entombed bodies, undisturbed for over a hundred years. Apartments haunted by former residents who died gruesome and mysterious deaths, and famous buildings where horrible and unspoken things happened behind closed doors. All are testaments to Richmond's brutal, bloody, and haunted past... and present.

The Edgar Allan Poe Museum

Edgar Allan Poe is often said to be "America's Shakespeare." The horror story, short story, lyric poetry, science fiction, and detective fiction are all formats he either mastered or created. For over 150 years adults and children alike have enjoyed his literature. Just a few blocks away from the Edgar Allen Poe Museum is Poe's first place of employment, the Southern Literary Messenger. His first Richmond home is also only a few blocks away from the museum.

The Edgar Allan Poe Museum is housed in a building known as the Old Stone House, the oldest original building in the city of Richmond. Jacob Ege owned the property in 1742 when the town was incorporated as a city by William Bryd II. Over the years the house has been the subject of many stories and is rumored to have been visited by several famous guests.

Edgar Allan Poe Museum. Photo Credit: Chayna Sellers.

James Monroe is said to have spent a night here during the Virginia Ratifying Convention of 1788. One of the Ege descendants recollected hearing the family talk about visits from Thomas Jefferson and James Madison. The house appears in postcards from the 1800s that said the Old Stone House served as headquarters for George Washington during the Revolutionary war, but we know Washington spent very little time, if any, in Richmond during the war so that claim is highly unlikely. However, Washington dispatched the Marquis de Lafayette to Richmond to prevent another attack on Richmond during the war and he was well-liked among Richmonders after winning the Battle of Petersburg. In 1824, the Marquis de Lafayette came back to Richmond with his son and visited the Old Stone House because the Ege family had helped supply Lafayette's troops during the Revolution. We know that a volunteer company of young Richmonders, the Junior Morgan Riflemen, rode in procession alongside Lafayette's carriage. One of the young riflemen was Edgar Allan Poe, then 15 years old and assigned to stand as honor guard outside the house during Lafayette's visit with the Ege family.

In the years to come, Poe would pass the house several times on his walks down Main Street to Rocketts Landing. He would have known of it since the house was already appearing in guidebooks as a Richmond landmark during Poe's life- time. An 1843 book already referred to the century-old house as "the Old Stone House" and called it the oldest house in Richmond.

Though Poe never lived in the building, it serves to commemorate his time living in Richmond. It is also a few blocks from the grave of his mother, Eliza Poe, at St. John's Church.

The Poe Museum and Enchanted Garden opened to the public in 1922. By the 1930s, the museum had already outgrown its original building and expanded into three adjoining structures. The third of these, the Elizabeth Arnold Poe Memorial Building, was constructed using a staircase taken from one of Poe's boyhood homes.

The museum devoted to the gothic author holds one of the world's largest col- lections of original manuscripts, letters, first editions, memorabilia and personal belongings. It also holds such interesting memorabilia as his socks and walking stick.

A dark shadowy figure is sometimes seen near Poe's walking stick and his wife's hand mirror. He's also seen in halls and gardens. On one occasion, he was captured in a photograph standing behind a tour group listening in on what the guide had to say. This shadow is believed to be the ghost of Edgar Allan Poe.

The garden is a popular venue for weddings and parties, and from time to time guests will inquire about the children they see playing in the corner of the garden during an event. When the children realize they've been spotted, they disappear. The two children most often appear in photographs that visitors have taken in the museum and gardens. They're likely the children of the property's original owners, although why they still haunt the garden remains a mystery.

The museum building houses the gift shop, front desk, and displays on the first floor, while the small rooms upstairs are used for storage. Museum staff frequent- ly report hearing footsteps overhead while working in the museum. One morning   a staff member walked upstairs and saw a small boy in the back bedroom dressed in knee length pants and a light-colored shirt. This young boy also enjoys playing in the gift shop. According to another staff member, a shipment of Edgar Allan Poe bobbleheads was left overnight in the shop ready to be unpacked the next day. However, the following morning the box had been unpacked and the figures lined up neatly on a shelf although the doors were locked from the night before.

Masons' Hall

In the early 1800s, Richmond's population was rising steadily. By 1860, the population reached nearly 38,000 making Richmond the largest city in Virginia and one of the biggest in the South. Few public buildings remain from the peri- od. A noteworthy exception is Masons' Hall. Built in 1788 to house Richmond's Masonic lodges, it is one of oldest continually used Masonic lodges in the world.

The Historic Freemasons Hall.

Masons' Hall is one of Richmond's most significant buildings. As one of the two largest meeting spaces in the early years of the city, Masons' Hall hosted the Richmond delegation to the Constitutional Convention, Rich- mond City Courts and Richmond City Council. It was opened not only for governmental func- tions, but also to religious groups that were unwelcome elsewhere. The building was a hospital during the War of 1812. The Marquis de Lafayette also stopped here on his 1824 tour and was made an honorary member. Eliza Poe, mother of Edgar Allen Poe, made her last performance as an actress here.

In order to be accepted into initiation into Mason membership and be ad- mitted into a "lodge" (which is technically a group of Mason's in a meeting, but also refers to the building they meet in), certain "requirements" have to be met, including but not limited to: Being a man, dedicating oneself to be- ing of sound mind and body, coming and asking to be admitted of your own free will or invitation, certifying that you are actually a "free man," i.e. not a slave, confirming that you have some belief in some kind of supreme being, that you allowed initiated Masons to conduct investigations confirming your assertions about your past, and claim to be committed to good morals and supporting your family and loved ones.

There are many interesting stories about Masons' Hall. One story is associated with the end of the Civil War. In April of 1865 the city was evacuated as the Union Army approached from the southeast along Williamsburg Road.. Chaos erupted and fires set to destroy military stores raged out of control and laid waste to much of the undefended city. The city fell prey to violence, looting and rioting. The elderly mayor, under a fluttering white sheet, approached the Union Army in a carriage with the urgent request for speed to advance and protect the citizens of the city. The Union Army advanced, restored order and extinguished the fires. Armed Union soldiers were immediately posted to protect three Richmond buildings, one of which was Masons' Hall. President Lincoln walked near Masons' Hall on his way to the Virginia Capitol on April 4, 1865, ten days before he was assassinated.

Masons' Hall is home to multiple spirits of the dead and not so gone. One of the building's caretakers admitted that he didn't believe in ghosts until an incident occurred on the third floor. He was alone in the building one night cleaning up after a meeting. He lined up the chairs along the wall, emptied the trash, and began vacuuming the meeting room. He suddenly felt a hand grab and squeeze his shoulder from behind and turned to see no one in the room. Since that incident, the caretaker said there's always a feeling up on the third floor like someone or something is there watching.

A paranormal group later investigated the room, which is normally set up as open space with chairs lined up against the walls. The investigators said they recorded a lot of activity in the third chair on the far wall of the meeting room, as well as heard several voices on an audio taping. A woman with the group sat in the third chair and she jumped up screaming. She told the team that she felt someone's hands on her throat.

A member of the Richmond Masons experienced the presence of something beyond the norm when he heard footsteps going up the stairs to the third floor. As the footsteps receded, there was a constant jingling of keys reminiscent of a jailor or caretaker with a ring of keys on a belt. The Mason decided to go up the stairs with another companion to investigate, but the stairs were eerily quiet and absent of any tangible presence. As they turned to go back down the stairs, the feeling of being followed was so real that they ran down the stairs without looking back.

Jefferson Park

Many locals would tell you if you're going to get to know Richmond, start at Jefferson Park, which overlooks the city highlighting the skyline and a vista that showcases some of the city's most historical and popular neighborhoods. The Peace Fountain, named after Alice Raisin—Richmond's "Ambassador of Compassion," is the park's central fountain and the centerpiece of Richmond's favorite overlook.

What locals won't tell you is that Jefferson Park is also a perfect example of how a city can have two sides, dueling personalities, things locals will brag about and things they will shrug off but make them look over their shoulder even in their own neighborhoods.

Jefferson Park.

The neighborhood this park overlooks, had a population in 1906 that was "all white except one negro family" according to applications to the National Historic District. Many properties were only sold to white owners because of deeds that barred contracts with persons of African descent. Other neighbor- hoods nearby, such as Woodville, were marketed to black owners as a "colored man's paradise."

While many of the ghosts of Richmond are connected to haunted history during colonial or civil war eras, the ghosts of Jefferson Park were, by most accounts, all products of tragic events and criminal undertakings of the twentieth century. Buried deep below the park, is the Church Hill train tunnel. One of Richmond's biggest disasters, and a site of tragic loss for the city, the tunnel was notoriously unstable. During construction, a section above the tracks once opened up and devoured an entire house from above. The most infamous story occurred in 1925 and gave birth to the legend of the Vampire of Richmond.

Much more recently, though, are the worst terrors that plagued Richmond in the 1980s and 1990s. None of these events were accidents, however, and they darkened the reputation of Richmond for decades causing a huge decline in its population several years running. Calling Richmond, and more specifically this 10-block radius, a war zone would not be an overstatement. In fact, in 1994, Richmond recorded an unprecedented 161 homicides in one year with 25 homicides just in the month of August, marking the bloodiest month of crime in the history of Richmond, with a homicide almost every day. In a year that had the Times- Dispatch writing an article that proclaimed a 10-day span with no murders as a victory, it seemed that any and every crime imaginable ended in death—from brazen robberies of jewelry stores that ended in a police shootout with deaths on both sides to a string of nursing home killings by a single man, Richmond killings made America's Most Wanted and the U.S. Postal Service finally had to be ordered back into dangerous neighborhoods by a Federal judge after refusing to deliver mail for a lengthy period of time.

The city was, perhaps, still traumatized by the string of almost a dozen robbery-murders by the Briley brothers in 1979. Ten victims ranging in ages from 5 to 79, were robbed and murdered over the course of seven months, with the Briley brothers using more than 10 different weapons to kill during their spree. While the details of the individual crimes are horrifying, even more terrifying was the dramatic prison riot and escape from death row along with a number of other death row inmates and conspirators in 1984. Were it not for the brave acts by their fellow death row inmates, the brothers would have raped and murdered a nurse, along with two other guards that they had doused in rubbing alcohol and intended to burn alive. Luckily for Richmond and Philadelphia (where the brothers escaped to), the police and the FBI tracked them and raided their uncle's house where they were hiding and sent them back to death row for a quick execution later that year. Even though it seemed the years of terror had finally ended with their executions, little did the city of Richmond know that they'd be back to haunt them in the afterlife.

Sadly, the victims of the Briley brothers, and the brothers themselves, are not the only ghosts said to haunt the Richmond and Jefferson Park area. Christopher Goines, the Boogie Man of Richmond, shot and killed a young family of five including his pregnant girlfriend. He then escaped Richmond and Virginia, leading the police and the FBI on a massive manhunt through four states all the way to New York. During that time, the Boogie Man of Richmond was featured on American's Most Wanted—showcasing Richmond for the second time in one decade in a very unfavorable light.

Walking through the park and seeing the view by day sometimes makes people forget what comes out at night. Sometimes, what sounds like a revving car followed by "whoops" and yells zooms by, but there is no car or any humans to be seen. Whispers are that it is the Briley brothers, riding back and forth around the park, looking for more crimes of opportunity, in death as they had done in life.

Another rumor, somehow even more horrible than the ghosts of the Briley brothers is what could be the source of other sounds that permeate the night in the park. One couple walking their dogs reported they heard crying deep into the park.

As they investigated, they saw a lone teenage girl sitting on a park bench, crying and holding her pregnant belly. It surprised them that a young pregnant girl was out so late by herself, even if the park is safer now than it has been in the past. As they approached her and asked her what was wrong, she looked up and said "I'm not ready yet. I'm just not ready." As they turned to get control of their dogs that started barking and perhaps call the police, they looked back and she was gone. Another lone jogger reported a similar story, but what distracted him was not dogs but five gunshots—the same amount of shots that Christopher Goines, the Boogie Man of Richmond, used to shoot each one of his victims one at a time in the head. The exception was his pregnant teenage girlfriend, on whom he used twice as many as other five victims put together. When the jogger looked back to the bench after the gunshots, the girl was gone, but he swore he could still hear weeping in the distance.

Pohlig Box Factory

Deep in the heart of Shockoe Bottom, one of Richmond's oldest neighborhoods, the Pohlig Box Factory building is one of the best-preserved antebellum warehouses still standing. Trying to preserve its historical architecture and personality, it wasn't altered much when it was converted to commercial apartments in the 1990s. The floors are heart pine in places, maple or stained concrete in others. Such artifacts as elevator cogwheels and massive sliding doors were reinstalled as decorations.

This unique and iconic building was not only used for multiple purposes and by several businesses but changed names as many times as it changed hands. Just some of names it has gone by are: Pohlig Box Company, A. Pohlig Paper Box Factory, Pohlig Bros. Inc, Turpin & Yarborough Tobacco Company, Turpin Factory Hospital, Yarborough Factory Hospital, & Second Alabama Hospital.

The Pohlig Box Factory.

Although the initial use for the building was as a tobacco company in 1853 when it was built, the warehouse soon served as a Civil War hospital only a few years later in 1861, and then became a box factory in 1909 and operated there until 1992.

The hospital, according to historical records, would not have been established without the patronage of Mrs. Juliet O. Hopkins, wife of noted Judge

Arthur F. Hopkins, who was instrumental in establishing two hospitals in the city.

Before the hospital ever opened its doors to the poor, wounded, and dying soldiers, Mrs. Hopkins was already busy recruiting and training nurses and hospital administration staff. Overseeing operations and fundraising, she organized everything from provision and supplies to receiving donations and eventually a steady flow of soldiers needing treatment from the front in Alabama.

Even still, over 300 soldiers drew their last breath in the building when it served as the makeshift hospital for the Second Alabama regiment. Soon after the conclusion of the Civil War the building was used as a Union prison hospital. Both Confederate and Union soldiers succumbed to death due to blood loss from musket injuries and traumatic blade wounds from unsuccessful amputations by inexperienced volunteer surgeons, or from infection after surviving either of the first two horrible fates. This, of course, lends credence that rumors of multiple spirits that supposedly remain there to this day, haunting visitors and residents alike. Some say it's the most haunted building in Richmond.

The ghost stories have done little to deter people from moving in and living amongst the spirits, and while many residents remain skeptical, the building management will readily share stories of what they think are confirmed super- natural encounters inside the building. According to these sources, one resident's young daughter woke up screaming in the middle of the night. When the noise disturbance was reported to management and they inquired about the incident, her father told them that all she could say was "Where did it go? Where did it go?!" She apparently had seen something like a dark figure in her room that disappeared as suddenly as it had appeared. Was it just an ordinary night- mare or was there a shadowy presence in the apartment, perhaps an apparition of a former soldier who died in suffering in pain in that very room?

One of the leasing agents still claims she doesn't believe in ghosts, despite the fact that one night in her very own apartment in the Pohlig Box Factory, she saw a   very distinct figure of a man stumbling through the hall towards the bedroom, with his hand on his head, moaning as if in pain. Still in disbelief, she yelled "Get out of my door!" and the figure disappeared, as if taking a command from one of his former officers.

If you believe the local legends that make their way around the neighborhood, they say that the whole building isn't haunted, just one unit in particular. It's whispered that angry spirits live in the most haunted apartment in the most haunted building in Richmond—Apartment 307. Whether or not the residents know or believe these rumors, locals and management are firm believers and avoid the spectral energy of this particular unit at all costs.

1719 E. Franklin St.

The oldest commercial building in Richmond dates back to 1817, when James Madison was the 4th President of the United States. Decades later, during the Civil War, embattled and exhausted soldiers of the Union Army finally walked down this street and passed by this very spot on their victory march into Richmond. The building was initially used as a lumber house and went through several incarnations before becoming Shockoe Whiskey and Wine for only a year before abruptly shutting down.

During that time, staff and patrons were convinced it was haunted, especially when the business failed, one in a long line of failing businesses, leaving locals to believe the building is cursed. Two former owners both swear the build- ing is haunted.One being the former owner of Shockoe Whiskey and Wine, who says the poor apprentice who died there still haunts the building as " just a scared kid" wandering the premises day or night.

1719 E. Franklin St.

In 1817, James McNaught was the man in Richmond to see about firearms. He was hailed as "the most celebrated gunsmith of this city" by the local press for the "uncommon excellence" of his firearms. Around this time, he took on an apprentice, 14-year-old Daniel Denoon. Daniel lost his father in the War of 1812 and was grateful for the opportunity to learn from such a skilled master.

Teacher and pupil quickly formed a close bond and for more than eight years, worked together in perfect trust and harmony. McNaught would even leave the shop in Denoon's hands for as many as nine months at a time while he visited England. By 1826, however, McNaught had grown upset by Daniel's repeatedly stated desire to set out on his own.

At 22 years old, Daniel already had stayed on for more than a year after his apprenticeship ended and was quietly disappointed at not receiving the bonus McNaught had promised him for running the operation during his long absence. McNaught's increasingly heavy drinking and lax business practices also were driving Daniel away.

But their relationship apparently remained harmonious until several weeks later, when after dinner with his family, foreman and apprentices, McNaught called Daniel upstairs.

As Denoon reached the top stair, McNaught coldly aimed a pistol at his protege's abdomen and fired. Then McNaught turned the gun on himself. Denoon was shocked and stupefied at his respected master's deeds, Denoon fell to the bottom of the steps and was barely able to describe the incident before expiring. McNaught survived, but in another fit of apparent madness he committed suicide while in the city jail.

To this day, the scene of the unjustified murder remains an unsettling place, with strange phenomena occasionally observed by employees and patrons of the previous businesses that occupied the former gun shop.

In 2003, the building's new owner began a remodeling project to replace the staircase Denoon fell down when he died. During renovations contractors struggled to restore the spiral staircase. The steps would sink every time and the project wouldn't pass inspection. They decided to tear out the staircase and build a stor- age closet in its place. Ever since strange noises and thumping sounds have been heard emanating from the space. Denoon fell down the staircase and succumbed to his wounds where the women's bathroom is today. Patrons and workers whis- per about an unusual cold spot and the strange sounds of something falling near the bathrooms. Even more horrifying are the experience women have had in the restroom. These poor women will be washing their hands, then look up and sud- denly see a young man in the mirror. When they spin around to yell and curse at the young peeping Tom, they're astonished to see no one is there. The opposite of a vampire with no reflection, this reflection has no body to go with it!

C&O Church Hill Tunnel

When the 4,000-foot-long Church Hill Tunnel was completed in 1873, it was one of the longest tunnels in the United States. The goal was to join the C&O tracks to the new Peninsula Subdivision railroad that would transport coal 75 miles southeast to Collis P. Huntington's new coal terminal at Newport News. But building the tunnel at this location, which involved channeling through soft wet clay and limestone, proved to be problematic from the start. At least nine men were killed by cave-ins at the tunnel from the beginning of its construction in the 1870s through the years of the coal flowing eastwards during its operation until 1925.

The Church Hill Tunnel, Eastern end.

On October 2, 1925, while the tunnel was undergoing repairs, a steam engine locomotive pulling 10 flat cars, entered the dark tunnel on its way to where it and its passengers would never see daylight again. As it neared the western entrance only 10 blocks from where it entered, the tunnel suddenly collapsed, trapping the train and killing a number of workers.

When the collapse happened, the men were in total darkness, with debris falling all around them. And a dangerous explosion building in the engine car. The laborers screamed and cried out desperately for help, some crawled under the flatbed trucks and escaped, but some never found their way out after a 190-foot stretch of tunnel buried them alive. Rail workers had been attempting to shore up the tunnel so it could finally be ready to stay open for active duty 24 hours a day. Unfortunately, their efforts resulted in the opposite scenario, a deadly collapse that would close the tunnel forever. Rescu- ers tried to reach the workers from both ends of the tunnel and from above, but were unable to locate the bodies of at least two laborers, Richard Mosby and H. Smith. When railroad officials decided that the tunnel had proven to be too dangerous and too costly, the entire stretch of cursed real estate—train and dead workers included—was sealed up with sand and concrete. The unclaimed bodies remain there to this day. When the surviving workers who inadvertently caused the collapse streamed out from the darkness of the tunnel, they yelled for joy, just happy to be alive and not trapped in the cursed tomb. When interviewed, some workers were too afraid to even speak of what happened. Others described the long run through complete darkness as some of the longest moments of their lives.

Even before the fateful collapse, the tunnel seemed to have a black spell upon it that caused tragedy after tragedy. During its 50-year construction and operation from 1880-1925, at least nine work- ers were killed, most likely more. In the months leading up to the final collapse in 1925, there were several small cave-ins, yet they still decided to continue the maintenance work and test fate by letting steam engines and train cars pass through.

Ever since the tunnel finally closed there have been multiple adventurers and explorers attempting to get inside and find the long-lost steam engine. In 1998, Richmond Times-Dispatch reporter, Mark Holmberg, and two others accompanied him through a breach in the concrete wall at the South end of the tunnel. Their attempt was as unsuccessful as that of the Virginia Histor- ical Society in 2003, when they joined forces with Richmond history lover and railroad tycoon, Pete Claussen, to try and discover a way to unearth the famous steam engine from its sealed tomb. All both parties were met with was a dismal rush of dark, swampy water that blocked all progress. After spending almost $5 million trying to reveal the tunnel's secrets, the effort by Pete Claussen was abandoned and no one has taken it up since, despite locals calling for the city to once and for all retrieve the train and laborers to give them a proper burial.

Most years in early October, residents of the nearby apartments sit unaware on a patio that has the moss-covered stone arch that hides the sealed en- trance to the tunnel as its back drop, they swear they hear a ghostly train whistle coming from the sealed-up tunnel. Other times, people have heard faint and muffled cries coming from the men who were trapped forever.

On that tragic day in October 1925, the Richmond Vampire made his first and last appearance. After the tunnel collapsed a bloody creature with jagged teeth and skin hanging from his body emerged from the wreckage. Some say the bloody creature made a run for it towards the James River and after being chased disappeared into the mausoleum of W. W. Pool in Hollywood Cemetery. The legends may be influenced by the architecture of the tomb, which has both Masonic and ancient Egyptian elements, and double W's looking like fangs. Only the year 1913 is etched over the entrance. Some believe not showing a birth and death date represent his immortality.

The Richmond Vampire was probably a case of mistaken identity with a 28-year old fireman working near the boiler of the train, which exploded in the collapse. His name was Benjamin Mosby, he survived the tunnel collapse, but was badly burned and had several broken teeth. He was in shock and made a run for the river before eventually being taken to Grace Street Hospital where he later died from his injuries and was buried in Hollywood Cemetery. Perhaps Mosby's shadow at his final resting place is the one people claim to see near W. W. Pool's mausoleum.

Patrick Henry's Pub and Grille

The Greek Revival townhouse at 2300 Broad Street was a wedding present built in 1850 by brickyard owner William Caitlin for Rebecca, his third wife.

This four-story Greek revival house has since been a brothel, a speak-easy, a family home and a private club. It now serves customers as the Patrick Henry Pub & Grille.

Patrick Henry's Pub and Grille.

A bartender who worked in the building for over 10 years says that everyone who works here has an experience with its ghostly residents. One night, after a 2 am closing, he was alone in the pub. He heard the distinctive noise of the swinging door that connects the kitchen to the hallway open and close. He looked up, but saw no one there. Frightened at what he saw he ran outside, seeing the door continue to swing out of the corner of his eye.

The bartender came to work the next day certain that the security cameras would have recorded a spirit. He said that on the video feed you can see him look up at the noise, and then run outside. The camera in the hallway of the bar, the one that's pointed towards the swinging door, was totally blank during that period of time. Not before, not after, but only during the time of the swinging bar doors, it was blank.

This type of paranormal activity has been reported elsewhere in the city. At the Poe Museum, the Enchanted Garden is a serene setting for special occasions, such as weddings. Guests have called the museum to let them know that their videos, which had no issues during the events, go black at times when the house comes into view, only to show a full picture again once the house is out of the frame.

St. John's Church

Historic St. John's Church was the first church built in the City of Richmond. It was originally the parish church of Henrico County and was established in 1611 at Dutch Gap, now the site of the current Henricus Historical Park in Chesterfield County south of the city on the James river. The church was moved to the Church Hill neighborhood of the city in 1746 after a tumultuous century and a quarter on its original site.

Historic St. John's Church.

As tensions grew between the colonies and Great Britain in the 1770s, Virginia held a series of meetings to organize its protests against Great Britain. In March 1775, the Second Virginia Convention was held here at the church. Patrick Henry, George Washington, Thomas Jefferson, Peyton Randolph and other prominent Virginians were delegates to the convention. St. John's Church was the only building in Richmond suitable to hold the delegates.

Here, Patrick Henry, lawyer, statesmen and Governor of Virginia embodied the spirit of the Revolution on March 23, 1775, with his words, "Give me liberty… or give me death!". His often quoted riposte was a rallying cry, but his focus and passion were in the face of a terrible burden at home.

Just as Lincoln had to endure the death of his sons during the war, and yet car- ried on, Patrick Henry too was tortured by the suffering of someone he loved—his wife and lifelong sweetheart, Sarah Henry. After giving birth to her sixth child in 1771, she was cursed with diseases of the mind, or "loss of reason," an affliction that was not received well in eighteenth century colonial times. As rumors grew of his wife being possessed by demons, he was forced to confine her to the cold, dark dungeon of their house on the plantation. Doctors went so far as to recommend a straight-dress, which came before the infamous straight-jacket.

It is said that when not acting the statesman throughout the colonies, he would return home and visit her using a secret back staircase leading down to the dungeon. He bore it well in public, but in private, he was tormented not only by his wife's suffering, but also by the spreading fear throughout the plantation of his wife's demons. Servants would no longer enter the house, and when she finally died, she was tossed into an unmarked grave—common practice for those "crazy" individuals taken by the devil.

Some might be forgiven for thinking that after Sarah's horrible last years, death, and lack of a burial, Henry had nothing else to live for. Others say it was her spirit with him at the church that inspired him to finish his speeches, ignite the colonies, and go on to be the Governor of Virginia at a crucial tipping point in the colonies' history. Regardless, Henry's timely resolutions passed by a narrow margin and the American Revolution began the following month when shots were fired at Lexington and Concord. Was this the spark that set the colonies ablaze for freedom? Some historians believe war was inevitable, but these patriotic giants at this specific location at this point in time set the colonies on their fateful course towards freedom.

As far as freedom goes, the same cannot be said of the four separate ghosts that are said to roam the church and graveyard. Some spirits get attached to a build- ing or place and stay there. One is James O'Neil. Not much is known about this man who died over two centuries ago in 1814 and is buried at St. John's Church. Interestingly, according to locals and paranormal investigators, he loves to have his picture taken. Photographs of a blurry man fitting his description have been passed around in ghost hunting circles for years.

Another ghost, seen sometimes visiting from the Henry's plantation home of Scotchtown, is none other than Sarah Henry. Sometimes laughing maniacally, other times banging on the door for someone to let her out—thinking she is still trapped in her dungeon prison. Finally, when some are listening to the story of Patrick Henry and his famous speech, there are whispers of a variation of his famous words, "Give me death…just give me death."

St. John's Church is also the final resting place for Daniel Denoon, the gun-smith's apprentice who haunts the building at 1719 E. Franklin St., and Eliza Poe, actress and mother of Edgar Allen Poe, who fell sick on the stage of Masons' Hall. George Wythe, the first law professor in the United States, and a delegate to the Continental Congress and signatory of the Declaration of Independence, is buried in the churchyard. Although the wife of George Wythe
is said to haunt his colonial home that still stands in historic Williamsburg (along with another ghost by the name of Lady Ann Skipwith), George Wythe himself is the spectral visitor that haunts these cursed and hallowed grounds, even though   he died in his own house—poisoned by his great nephew, who was impatient to receive his inheritance. However, yellow arsenic was a slow-acting poison and George Wythe ended up writing his nephew out of the will just before dropping dead. His spirit is said to have followed his body here to St. Johns Church and can be seen writing at the podium, disappearing, and then reappearing again with his mouth open as if he is giving a speech. Is it the Declaration of Indepen- dence he is signing? What is he saying to his new audience of the twentieth century? One can only guess...

Rosie Connolly's

This prominent building was built in the early 1900s and was known as the Railroad YMCA Building. Shockoe Bottom in the early years of the last century was a place of questionable morals, practically the red-light district of Richmond. Several brothels were in the neighborhood, and the whiskey bars of Broad Street led to all sorts of distractions for the local youth and many well-meaning visitors brought in by the railroad.

The "Butchertown Cats," a gang that ruled the area that stretched from Shockoe Bottom to Church Hill, was best avoided unless you were actually looking to visit the back alley brothels or pay a visit to one of the many butchers with swinging meat. Naturally there was much objection to the immoral behavior that was happening down by the river.

Rosie Connolly's.

In 1872, the first Railroad YMCA was organized in Cleveland, Ohio, as a partnership between the YMCA and railroad companies to provide wholesome overnight lodging and meeting spaces for railroad workers.

That idea was taken up by the railroad company in Richmond, which was run by God-fearing men who had strong moral compasses and very involved Wives. Together they cooked up a scheme whereby the fourth floor of the railroad building head house was devoted to activities run by the YMCA, speech giving, sportsmanship, and scholastic achievement.

Two major railroad companies, the Seaboard Air Line (SAL) Railroad and the Chesapeake and Ohio (C&O) Railroad, had lines running through Richmond's Main Street Station, and put funds together to build the Richmond Railway YMCA building. It served as a YMCA until 1971 and currently houses residential apartments upstairs, the Old City Bar venue on the front, and nestled into the back cellar of the building is Rosie Connolly's, a family-owned pub famous for its beer and whiskey and its motto "Beer foam is why God gave us sleeves." But there have been reports of additional ghostly hands trying to help in the kitchen.

One afternoon, the family was preparing to open for the day and one of the daughters came out of the kitchen with a terrified look on her face. She said she saw a strange man in the kitchen and when she gave him a second glance, he quickly disappeared. The family shrugged it off until a few weeks later something similar happened in the kitchen.

Another one of the owner's daughters was cleaning up in the kitchen while waiting for a friend. She sensed someone watching her and assumed it was her friend. When she turned to look at her friend, she was startled to see a man she didn't recognize staring back at her. As soon as the shock registered, the man was gone.

The next time the daughter saw the man, she decided to confront him. "I was just about to give him a piece of my mind, but he vanished right around the corner and when I went after him he was nowhere to be seen." she said.

Later on, a server, who knew of the two ghostly encounters, was alone in the kitchen one evening. She turned from her duties to see a woman in an old-fash- ioned dress standing and looking, as if at a mirror. The spirit did not move as the server looked on and, recalling that the man would vanish, the server turned away and looked back, but the woman in the dress was still standing there appearing to look in the mirror. The server left to bring back a family member to witness the scene, but by the time she returned the mysterious woman had vanished.

None of the staff has had the feeling of being watched or witnessed ghostly sights in the dining room or the bar, but perhaps that's because those areas are addi- tions to the original building. The kitchen of the restaurant is well inside what would have been the old YMCA building. Unfortunately, there are few historical

details on the inhabitants of this building so we're not sure how to explain the identity of the ghosts. As the mission of the YMCA is to provide a safe space for people, perhaps these shadows felt safe in the building.

Lumpkin's Slave Jail

There is something about physically standing at a site where unspeakable trauma and great tragedy occurred. Sometimes the paranormal isn't observed by sight or sound, but by feeling. Think about that if you ever pass through this area of Shockoe Bottom.

Shockoe Bottom was the center of Richmond's slave trade. Auction houses, offices, slave jails, and residences of the most prominent slave traders were scattered throughout this section of Shockoe Bottom. Various historians have estimated that as many as 350,000 men, women and children were sold and sent south through Richmond.

Lumpkin's Slave Jail.

Much of Shockoe Bottom has since been razed and paved over. Nevertheless, this area of Shockoe Bottom remains sacred ground associated with suffering, injustice, and resistance to slavery.

The infamous Goodwin's Jail, a holding place for the real-life Solomon North- up (whose experiences were chronicled in the movie 12 Years a Slave) was in Shockoe Bottom.

Another major holding center for enslaved people was Lumpkin's Jail, known among those who experienced the horror or staying there as the "Devil's Half-Acre."

In 2008, an excavation of Lumpkin's Jail revealed an unexpectedly rich trove of artifacts — preserved buildings, clothing, ceramics, including a porcelain doll, and more — that archaeologists believe is only the beginning. The moist soil in Shockoe Bottom had stopped the growth of harmful bacteria, resulting in remarkably intact items.

Slaves fresh off the ships were held here before being sold on to plantations in the South or further west, or if they had been insolent or tried to escape they were punished here. One of the thousands who were held here described the condi- tions, "On the floor of the main room were iron rings, my hands and feet were stretched out, I was face down on the floor, spread-eagled and a large white man stood over me and he flogged me."

One spirit that lingers in this area is of Gabriel, a literate enslaved black-smith who planned a large slave rebellion in the late summer of 1800. On the day of the revolt, disaster struck. A large summer thunderstorm moved in and drenched the city. It took out bridges, cut off communication, and made it impossible for the revolt to begin. Gabriel tried to get word out that they would postpone until the following night. In the meantime, Gabriel was betrayed. Two enslaved men at a neighboring plantation lost their nerve and confessed to the owner.

The storm had cleared by the next morning, and roving white patrols picked up and detained dozens of conspirators. By the time they came for Gabriel, he was gone. Over the next few weeks, at least 10 conspirators were tried and hanged, including Gabriel's two older brothers. In the end, 26 were sentenced to death. Gabriel was eventually caught and hanged above the flat stones here on October 10 at the age of 24.

Historians believe Gabriel was buried at the African Burial Ground at 15th and Broad Streets in Richmond after his execution in 1800. Every year on October 10, there is a gathering to commemorate the day the great rebellion was executed at the town gallows in Richmond's African Burial Ground.

This desolate area, basically a field between a highway and the train tracks is rich in the ghosts of our collective past, haunted by the memories of our nations original sin.

African Burial Ground

The tunnel under Broad Street from the Lumpkin's Slave Jail leads to the African Burial Ground, which was used from around 1750 to 1816 as a cemetery for Richmond's free and enslaved black population. In unmarked graves, untended, perhaps lie hundreds or thousands of people. Relatives and forebears of millions across America today.

The land is charged with an energy that demands silence and contemplation of man's capacity for evil to other men.

African Burial Ground.

Both freemen and slaves, men women and children, all African American, were buried here for years. Then the city grew, and needed the land, houses were built here, houses doomed to be haunted. But the houses were for poor people and no records of their hauntings survive. Then Interstate 95 was built through the city, covering much of the graveyard site under 18 feet of earth and rubble.

The site was, for a long time, a car park, the graves paved over with rough asphalt. The staff and students of Virginia Commonwealth University left their cars on top of the graves for years. It wasn't a popular car park, out of the way, not well lit and literally vibrating with the ghosts of the thousands of souls under the dark black surface. The tireless work of local activists over many years has finally led to change.

The city now owns the land and the asphalt was eventually removed after a morning vigil by protestors on April 13 2011, which was timed for the day the first shot of the Civil War was fired 150 years ago. Four protestors were arrested, and the publicity served well to motivate action.

Plaques now are in place and the area is grassed over. The tunnel that joins the site to the Lumpkin's Slave Jail site under Broad Street is said to be paved with the stones from the hanging place on the African Burial Ground. Gabriel the salve could have stood on those stones before he was hung.

Richmond has slowly started to turn and face it's unsavory past. The Slave Trail is a historic walk along the path from the Manchester Docks, where thousands of slaves disembarked from the cramped, crowded holds of the ships that brought them to the New World. In the blinding light they were marched along the shore, across the Mayo Bridge and to Lumpkin's Jail where they would await their sale day, as the need for slaves in Richmond had diminished with the plantation industry, they often went further south and west.

The Slave Trail finishes at the African Burial Ground near the 2007 Richmond Reconciliation Statue. The statue is on the other side of the freeway from Lumpkin's Slave Jail, at the corner of 15th and Main Streets. Identical statues were also installed in Liverpool, England, and the Republic of Benin in West Africa in memory of the triangular route of the slave trade. Villagers were kidnapped in West Africa, taken to the New World to grow cotton, sugar and tobacco, which was then taken back to Europe to be sold and made into rum, textiles and other manufactured goods that were taken back and sold in West Africa.

The future for the site is uncertain, but there have been plans for a museum on the site to talk about the slave trade and its importance to Richmond and its effects on today's society.

Monumental Church

On the corner of Broad and 14th Streets stood the Richmond's first theatre, a barn-like building that opened its doors on October 10, 1786. A previous building at the same location was known initially as the first Academy of Fine Arts and Sciences in America, and subsequently the site has been known as "The Theatre Square."

Monumental Church.

Many important actors of the day performed in the theater, including Eliza Poe. She gave her final performance not here, but at the nearby Masons' Hall. She died of consumption in early December of 1811, a few weeks before a fire at the Richmond Theatre claimed the lives of over 72 people, including the Governor at the time, Mr. George William Smith.

More than 600 people attended the performance on December 26, 1811. This was a big crowd in Richmond in 1811, almost 6% of the city's total pop- ulation at the time. The fire started during an encore performance when an oil lamp in a chandelier brushed against one of the cloth backdrops. The fire was mostly hidden from the audience as it spread beyond control. In fact, when small burning pieces of the ceiling began to fall onto the stage, the audience thought it was part of the production. It's only when an actor yelled "The house is on fire" that chaos erupted in the theater as 600 people attempted to escape. Within 10 minutes of the start of the fire, the entire building was in flames.

The victims who lost their lives in the fire of 1811 are still buried within Monumental Church, the building that replaced the theatre and was dedicated to honor them in 1814,. The names of those known to have perished are engraved under the entrance portico of the Church. Many of the bodies found in the ashes could not be identified or collected as many of the bones turned to dust. The unidentified remains were gathered together and were later enclosed in two mahogany boxes in the vault below the portico of the newly built church.

Constructed on the site of the razed Theatre in 1814, Monumental Church was designed by Robert Mills, America's first native born architect and pupil of Thomas Jefferson. It's an unusual octagonal design with an elegant dome at the center. Mills designed several churches topped with the Delorme dome (inspired by a similar feature at Monticello, in turn inspired by a dome seen by Jefferson in Paris), but Richmond's Monumental Church is the last surviving example in the nation.

Often after tragedies such as this, we often sadly learn about premonitions that people experienced beforehand. One story was passed down from a Mrs. McRae to her granddaughter. The story is about a girl named Nancy Green, who had been adopted into the family of Patrick Gibson. Nancy's birthday was on December 27 and she was about to turn 16. Nancy's biological father, J.W. Green, was scheduled to perform at the Richmond Theater on December 26. That morning, Mrs. Gibson asked Nancy to run an errand
a few blocks away. The Gibson house was on Leigh Street between 7th and 8th Streets where there was a deep ravine running under the street. When she returned home from her errand, Nancy had lost color in her face and reported to Mrs. Gibson that she heard a ghost calling to her from the ravine. The ghost chanted "Nancy, Nancy, Nancy Green, you'll die before you are sixteen." Nancy was understandably upset and refused to go to the theater that night. Mrs. Gibson calmed her down and convinced Nancy to go to the theater out of respect for her father. Mrs. Gibson, Nancy, and Mrs. McRae went to the theater that evening. When the fire broke out, Mrs. McRae was on the second

floor of the building and escaped by jumping out of the window. Unfortunately, Mrs. Gibson and Nancy did not make it out of the building. The prophecy of the ghost in the ra- vine had come true, Nancy did not live to see her 16th birthday.

There have been several ghost stories associated with the Richmond Theatre fire of 1811. Many church workers and paranormal experts have confessed to having eerie experiences at Monumental Church. There have been voices heard com- ing from the balcony of the church and unexplained noises as well. Many of the doors slam shut without anyone being around them and some of the doors will open and close seemingly of their own will.

Church workers have told stories of leaving their tools in one spot, only to have the tools disappear and reappear in a completely different place. Caretakers have mentioned that motion detectors have gone off at random times without a person in sight. Some workers have heard heavy footsteps in the church and it is said that some of them were so scared, that they never returned to Monumental Church.

Virginia State Capitol

The Virginia State Capitol, which Thomas Jefferson designed with Charles-Lou- is Clérisseau, was the first Roman Revival building in America and the first American public building in the form of a classic temple.

Construction on the Capitol building began in 1785 and it was finished 13 years later. Major historical moments took place in the building, such as the ratifica- tion of the Bill of Rights in amendment to the United States Consti- tution in 1791 and the vote to secede from the Union in April 1861.

The Virginia State Capitol.

On April 27, 1870, during arguments before the Virginia Supreme Court of Appeals about a hotly disputed Richmond mayoral election, the balcony of the third-floor courtroom of the Capitol building collapsed. The floor of the court- room crashed into the chamber of the House of Delegates one floor below. More than 60 people died in what came to be known as the Capitol Disaster.

A news article from 1870 reported "hundreds of persons in the Capitol Square are weeping and wailing as the dead and dying are brought out of the building." Despite some calls to raze and replace the damaged Capitol, the legislators approved funds and repaired the building. Sometimes when people die in an accidental disaster they can't let go of the pain and terror they felt before dying. Security officers who work in the building at night say that they occasionally hear muffled shrieks and moans echo through the calls when it's very quiet. Most of the activity comes from the basement below the room where the delegates chamber used to reside until extensive renovations at the turn of the twentieth century.

It's easy to believe these frightening sounds would be the paranormal mani-festa- tions of the tragedy repeated throughout the decades.

Virginia Governor's Mansion

The Virginia Governor's Mansion, also known as the Executive Mansion, is actually the oldest governor's mansion in the United States that is still occupied. The Executive Mansion changes residents every few years based on Election Day results, but some say there's at least one guest who never leaves.

Capitol Police officers stand guard along the mansion walls and sometimes see light coming from the building when they know the first family of Virginia is away. They say you can actually watch someone walking upstairs with a candle going from room to room. There are also reports of a number of strange occurrences happening in the house including paintings moving, lights refusing to turn off even when the switch is flipped.

The mansion has been in service since 1813 and reports of it being haunted began as early as the 1890s when the governor of the time, Philip McKinney, saw the apparition of a young woman sitting by the window. The same apparition has been seen a number of times over the years by a variety of witnesses including police officers who also say they hear footsteps and the rustling taffeta dress through the halls.

According to the Executive Mansion docent manual, 150 years ago there was a party at the mansion. Because of the icy weather, the first family invited a young woman in a long taffeta ball gown to stay overnight. When she departed early the next morning, her carriage overturned, and she died. Some say her youthful spirit returned her to the last place she felt joy.

Governor's Mansion. Library of Congress Prints and Photographs Division.

GHOSTFLIX

Join Ghost Experiences and Tours Everywhere...Anytime.

Embark on ghost experiences and tours of over 25 cities
across the US. Watch on-demand, or join live events!

New Orleans Ghosts
New Orleans, LA

DC Ghosts
Washington, DC

Asheville Terrors
Asheville, NC

Sit back, eat some snacks, and enjoy both live streaming and pre-recorded guided ghost tours and experiences at home with GhostFlix, a streaming platform that lets viewers join tour guides through the streets of 25 cities across the US while listening to their eerie ghost stories and haunted histories.

Exploring a city through ghost stories shared by locals is a great way to uncover its hidden culture and storied past. From the River Monster of Gatlinburg to the Head Boiler of San Antonio, ghost tours answer the first question you should ask in any place: Is it haunted?

Ghostflix offers a variety of experiences, and we're always adding new content. GhostFlix tours walk you through the streets to 8 haunted historic locations around the Crescent City from the comfort of your own home, or the eerie streets of Salem, Massachusetts, where you'll hear stories of the witch trials and other hauntings.

Join us for these and other ghostly adventures on usghostadventures.com/ghostflix

Portland Ghosts
Portland, OR

LA Ghosts
Los Angeles, CA

Civil War Ghosts
Gettysburg, PA

Boston Ghosts,
Boston, MA

"I am addicted lol... I have booked for every walk. I love how all the tour guides are friendly and I feel like I am walking along beside them.... Thank you for doing these ghost tours it is helping with me not being able to travel. You all are bringing it to me and I truly appreciate it..." - Lana

Colonial Ghosts
Williamsburg, VA

Union Station, circa 1914.

CHAPTER III - PART 1

The Ghosts of Washington, D.C.

The notion of ghosts may be difficult enough to comprehend and believe, but paranormal experts take it a step further and try to understand why these ghosts are here. In general, they stay for one of two reasons or sometimes for both.

The first reason involves a traumatic or tragic sudden ending that leaves the spirit unable to move on because of anger, sadness, longing or some other powerful emotion. The second involves the idea that unfinished business compels a spirit to remain.

Because Washington, D.C. is at the heart of the nation, both reasons have led to its many ghosts who haunt buildings and parks that are so ingrained into the psyche of the nation. It's home of our capital since July 16, 1790 and has been a magnet for passionate, ambitious and powerful people ever since. The potential for high emotions and unfinished business is magnified. Take the case of Commodore Barron, stripped of his naval command by Stephen Decatur and teased for it by the very same man. No wonder the two ended up dueling, where all things seemed to be legal, New Jersey. The end was as you can imagine, emotional.

The Treasury Annex

Stories about a ghostly woman who appears suddenly, stares at late-night workers, turns transparent and then vanishes have been told by many people at the Treasury Annex.

Who is she? Why is she attached to this building and why can't she leave? She is perhaps Anna Durren who was a mid-level office manager during the 1970s and who famously ran a tight ship. Long after her shift had ended, Anna continued to bark orders at her assistants. She was addicted to her job and for a single woman with no friends, it was all she had to occupy her time. Yet after years of work, she descended into madness and her colleagues remember her pacing her office in a manic state, reciting long strings of numbers and tax codes. She was eventu- ally forced to resign, and that was the last anyone heard of Anna Durren until her ghost appeared.

The Treasury Annex.

Current employees working the night shift at the Annex report hearing strange mumbling from vacant office rooms. If they concentrate hard enough, it sounds like the recitation of financial documents and tax forms.

Lafayette Square

Lafayette Square, a seven-acre plot of land, was originally named President's Park and was intended as the recreational grounds for the White House.

In 1924, President's Park became Lafayette Square, named after the French offi- cer, Gilbert du Motier, the Marquis de Lafayette. This "Hero of Two Worlds," as he was called, fought for the Colonies during the American Revolution and then later fought in the French Revolution. It seems fitting that the park was named for a man steeped in war, bloodshed and destruction.

Lafayette Square was once a racetrack where men gambled, generally a place of ill repute. Vagabonds, their breath smelling of moonshine, would corner a person against a tree or hide in the shadows and wait for the right opportunity to grab a wallet.

Lafayette Square.

The Square was also used as a slave market. Many park goers have heard the shrill screams of young children being torn from their families. The young kids will run up to adults in the park, hoping to find surrogate parents.

The ghost of Philip Barton Key, the son of Francis Scott Key of "The Star-Span- gled Banner" fame, often appears here. Philip Key was an influential lawyer and, as a widower, one of the most eligible bachelors in the social cir- cles of Washing- ton, D.C. in the 1850s. His fate was sealed when he began an affair with Teresa Sickles, the young trophy wife of Senator Dan Sickles. After years of neglect and abuse from Sickles, Teresa hoped to find love with Philip Key and it wasn't long before they were involved in a passionate affair. They did not worry as the senator had countless affairs of his own. Yet when he discovered his wife's affair, he was incensed.

Even after forcing Teresa to write a confession that ruined her reputation, Sickles was still enraged. On the morning of February 27, 1859, he saw Philip Key in Lafayette Square and cried out, "Key! You have dishonored my home and must die!" With that he pulled out his Colt revolver and shot the unarmed lawyer several times until Key lay dead.

Sightings of Philip Key's ghost began as early as Senator Sickles' trial. Sickles was the first person to successfully argue he was not guilty because of temporary insanity. Late in the evening after the verdict was read, passers-by said they saw a ghostly figure shouting at the courthouse denouncing its unjust ruling.

Since that day, Philip Key's ghost has been seen often. Some believe he's calling out to his love, hoping he'll find Teresa Sickles. Numerous women in their early twenties have reported being followed from Lafayette Square, never seeing the apparition but hearing footsteps and even feeling a soft touch on the shoulder.

There are others who say the ghost doesn't call for love but instead for justice. They do not report a soft touch but instead a swift yank. The tragic story of Philip Barton Key has become legendary as more than a thousand firsthand witnesses have experienced his presence.

The White House

The White House was built largely by enslaved and free African American laborers, burned in the War of 1812 by British Troops, and then reconstructed from 1815 to 1817. It has been the home of every United States president since 1800.

Many believe that the ghost of the inaugural First Lady of the White House, Abigail Adams, feels a sense of ownership and responsibility. The first appear- ances of her ghost sprang up soon after her death in 1818. In 1974, a helicopter stolen from a military base landed on the White House grounds. Nobody was hurt, but staff reported sightings of Abigail's apparition on that day. Twenty years later, she appeared again. On that second occasion, an ultra-light aircraft entered the grounds and mysteriously crashed, killing the pilot. Secret Servicemen remember an older woman fitting Abigail's description directing emergency response teams attending the accident.

The White House at night.

Of the many ghosts who wander the White House, the most famous is, of course, Abraham Lincoln. In fact, there have been so many Lincoln sightings that he is known as "The White House Ghost." And these sightings are from some of the world's most famous figures. Theodore Roosevelt saw Lincoln's ghost, as did First Lady Grace Coolidge. Staying at the White House, Winston Churchill awoke and walked to the adjoining bathroom not wearing a stitch of clothing. When the two crossed paths he said, in typical Churchill style, "Mr. President, you have me at a disadvantage." President Lincoln laughed and disappeared. Eleanor Roosevelt felt his presence and noted that her dog barked at what appeared to be nothing. President Truman and his daughter both heard knocking on the Lincoln Bedroom door.

For three nights before he was killed, Lincoln had dreams about being assassi- nated. These dreams troubled him, and he told them to his biographer and to his bodyguard, William Crook. On the fateful evening instead of saying, "Good- night Crook," as he ordinarily did, Lincoln said, "Goodbye Crook." But after his death he tried to warn other presidents. On November 19, 1963, three nights before John F. Kennedy was assassinated, Jackie Kennedy remembered find- ing a black top hat on their dresser, the same iconic hat that Honest Abe always wore. And the next day Jackie told an assistant how she thought it was odd that a Secret Serviceman was carrying a nineteenth century Deringer—the same pistol used by John Wilkes Booth to assassinate Lincoln.

Although J.F.K. did not escape his fate, Mr. Lincoln's ghost worked to im- prove his warnings. In early May 1979, President Jimmy Carter was preparing to give a speech at the Civic Center Mall in Los Angeles when he found a newspaper sprawled across his desk with a headline regarding Lee Harvey Oswald. It gave President Carter an uneasy feeling, and his intuition told him to increase security at the mall. Sure enough, ten minutes before Carter began his speech, the Secret Service arrested a man coincidentally named Raymond Lee Harvey who was carrying a pistol and who was involved in an assassination plot.

Blair House

On November 1, 1950, two men with guns entered the grounds in front of Blair House. These men had come to assassinate President Truman. Griselio Torresola and Oscar Collazo were Puerto Rican nationalists who considered the U.S. and Puerto Rico to be at war. Blair House, at the time, was the temporary residence of President Harry Truman because the interior of the White House was being renovated.

But things did not go as planned. In a furious 40-second attack, Torresola was killed and Collazo was seriously wounded in a gunfight with police officers. Since that day Torresola's savage soul has taken up permanent residence at the Blair House, also known as the President's Guest House.

Blair House, near the White House.

The house was originally built in 1824 for Surgeon General Joseph Lovell but was later acquired by newspaper magnate and political activist Francis Preston Blair in 1836. Blair was a close friend of President Andrew Jackson; his newspa- per, the Globe, was essentially a propaganda sheet for the pres- ident. However, it was Blair's status as part of Andrew Jackson's "Kitchen Cabinet," the group of advisors he relied on after dismissing his official Cab- inet, that may have attract- ed various ghosts who disliked Jackson. Jackson had offended many during his long military career.

Now, almost two hundred years later, the house still harbors a dark ener- gy. Many famous visitors to the President's Guest House, including Queen Elizabeth II, Winston Churchill, Margaret Thatcher, and even Vladimir Putin have described their stays as being "confusing," "hazy," or "draining." It is as though the faint outline of an unknown man follows a guest from room to room.

The Decatur House

The Decatur House is one of the oldest homes in Washington, D.C. It was constructed in 1818 for naval hero Stephen Decatur and his wife. Today it is a museum showcasing African American history.

Some visitors have complained of stomach pains during and after their tour. They might wonder if they have a virus or are suffering from food poisoning. And their doctor will not be able to provide an explanation. Many believe that these stomach pains are due to the paranormal influence of the ghost of Stephen Decatur. He died in his bedroom after being shot in the abdomen during a duel with Commodore James Barron. He suffered in agony for two days before he died.

Commodore Barron wanted Decatur dead. He blamed Decatur for his role in stripping Barron of his naval command years earlier. James Barron commanded the U.S.S. *Chesapeake*, and when it was attacked by the British H.M.S. *Leopard*, Barron offered almost no resistance and surrendered. The British were after deserters and tried four sailors on the *Chesapeake*, hanging one and sentencing the others. The event was humiliating for the young United States, and as a result of his cowardice and poor leadership, Barron was stripped of duty for five years. Stephen Decatur had been a member of the jury that convicted him.

The Decatur House.

In 1820, after years of bitterness, Barron tracked Decatur down and challenged him to a duel. Then James Barron mortally wounded Decatur. After three attempts at sewing the wound, Decatur's blood soaked through all the bed sheets. It is said that Decatur shouted out, "I did not know that any man could suffer such pain!" Finally, the Commodore succumbed to his wounds, after which his wife became hysterical and had to be sedated. She never fully recovered from her husband's loss.

Decatur's ghost appeared almost immediately after his death. He is often seen gazing out the upstairs window, watching the street as if anticipating the arrival of Barron. The apparition appeared often, causing the window to eventually be walled up. Others still catch a glimpse of him in the early hours leaving through the back door with pistols in hand.

The Hay-Adams Hotel

Visiting Presidents and other guests of the country often stay at the Hay-Adams Hotel which has a suitably high level of style and elegance.

Before 1928, when the Hay-Adams Hotel was built, two beautiful Victorian homes stood on the site. One of the homes was owned by the Hay family, and the other by the Adams family. John Hay was the personal secretary of Abraham Lincoln, and Henry Adams was a successful author and the grandson of John Quincy Adams.

On a December morning in 1885, Henry Adams left his house for a dentist ap- pointment. But before he could walk through Lafayette Square, he met a family

The Hay-Adams Hotel.

friend who wanted to pay a visit to his wife, Mrs. Marian Hooper Adams, who was known as Clover. Mr. Adams then delayed his appointment and escorted his wife's friend back to their home.

But when he returned and went up the stairs, his wife was found lying on the floor in front of her fireplace. An empty vial of potassium cyanide, which she used for her amateur photography, lay next to her hand. Adams picked up his wife and brought her to the sofa and then sent for a doctor. But it was too late; she was dead.

Some say she was depressed over the death of her father, while others say she felt lonely and neglected by a husband who seemed to love the esteem of the world more than the esteem of his wife. Some people even hinted that she didn't kill herself but instead was killed by Henry Adams.

Adams responded by burning all her possessions, destroying any evidence. Rumors were rampant that he had a mistress and that his strange silence after her death was more than just an attempt to avoid old memories.

Yet, almost from the day the two old houses were razed, and the Hays-Adams Hotel was erected, staff and guests have reported paranormal happenings. Doors open and close mysteriously. Radios turn on and off. The sounds of a weeping woman have filled the halls. These phenomena occur in the first few weeks of December, around the anniversary of Clover's death.

Many famous guests have stayed at the hotel, such as Amelia Earhart and Charles Lindbergh. Amelia Earhart disappeared while attempting to set another record as a female pilot. Charles Lindbergh suffered through the kidnapping and murder of his infant son. Some believe they were cursed by the Clover's ghost. The connection may be that both famous guests sought the esteem of the world and were adored by fans, just like Clover's emotionally distant husband. And both guests stayed at the hotel on the first Sunday of December. It was on this day, that Clover Adams drew her last breath. Could she have taken more than just despair and sadness with her to the grave, but vengeance and rage as well? The staff knows the doors don't just open and close on the first Sunday. They slam. Some of the oldest staff members say that particular night is a cursed time to stay in the Hay-Adams Hotel.

St. John's Episcopal Church

St. John's Episcopal Church is the second oldest structure in Lafayette Square. It famously rings its bells in honor of a president, ex-president or other notable person when they pass away. These bells were heard when Ronald Reagan and Gerald Ford died.

The bell weighs more than a thousand pounds and was cast by the Revere Com- pany of Boston, the company founded by Paul Revere's son. Its characteristic chime echoes throughout the park as a final send off.

St. John's is known as the President's Church. Every president since James Madison has attended the church at least occasionally. The church always has a pew reserved for the president. When James Madison was president, the pew was numbered 28. Although the pew has been renumbered due to various renova- tions, the same pew is still reserved for the current president but is now num- bered 54.

St. John's Episcopal Church.

After every president's death since the late 1800s, when the bell rang, the presi- dent's pew would mysteriously fill at midnight with six pale, spectral figures, men dressed in white robes. Witnesses throughout the years all de- scribed the same thing: these ghosts, who some call "The Great Washingto- nians," appear at the stroke of midnight to pay their respects and then vanish into thin air.

Who are these men? Some believe they are important but unsung Founding Fathers, six faceless heroes who never got the fame of a George Washing- ton, Thomas Jefferson, Paul Revere, or Patrick Henry. They were men who fought to protect our country, and they want to show respect for those who later were in charge.

Many believe these six figures in white robes feel a need to welcome to the after- life every leader of the great nation they all had a part in creating.

The Dolley Madison House

The Dolley Madison house has had more reports of ghostly sightings than any other place in Washington, D.C., except for the White House.

Dolley Madison, First Lady to President James Madison, was a woman who defined the role with a social grace, outgoing personality and sincere care for all people. As First Lady she dramatically boosted the popularity of her husband. Years earlier she had performed certain lady-like social duties for President Thomas Jefferson because he was a widower. And during the War of 1812, while the White House was burning, she rescued a portrait of George Washington.

The Cutts Madison House.

The latter half of her life was not as pleasant. When James Madison died in 1836, she moved into the Dolley Madison house and left the affairs of her planta- tion in her son's hands who quickly bankrupted the family. Through it all, Dolley displayed the same grace. People like Daniel Webster would secretly find ways
to help her without damaging her pride. Even an ex-slave of Madison's gave her money from his own pocket, pretending to still be paying for his freedom though he'd purchased it years before.

Is it any wonder that Dolley Madison's spirit wants to remain in a place where she was loved and when she was most vulnerable? After her death in 1849, the home was purchased by Rear Admiral Charles Wilkes, who covered up Dolley's favorite porch, replacing it with a window. Since then passersby often do a dou- ble take, because they believe they've seen Dolley sitting at the window just like she used to sit on the porch. Although she has also been seen at the White House, the Rose Garden and the Octagon House, she always seems most comfortable in her own home.

Occidental Grill

The Occidental Grill opened in 1908 and immediately became popular among politicians, dignitaries, sports stars, and celebrities. It was built by Henry Willard, who also built the Willard Hotel next door. Everyone from John F. Kennedy and Winston Churchill, to Steven Spielberg and Amelia Earhart has eaten at the Occidental Grill.

And they weren't just eating. Nuclear war may even have been prevented. In 1962, ABC News correspondent John Scali met with a mysterious Russian informant, then known only as Mr. X, although we now know it was Aleksandr Fomin, counselor at the Soviet Embassy. During their meeting, Fomin passed Scali some documents that confirmed the Russians were willing to make a deal during the Cuban Missile Crisis.

Some people who have eaten here loved it so much that they never stopped coming. For example, Teddy Roosevelt and Amelia Earhart, have been seen at a table, walking through the restaurant, or sitting at the bar.

Most of the employees agree, however, that it doesn't get really strange until after closing. Miguel, a dishwasher in the early 2000s, remembered one such encounter. He and the manager were straightening up the bar and sweeping up in the main dining room. Miguel remembered seeing a man at the bar out of the corner of his eye. When he turned, he saw a heavyset man in a dark suit, perched on one of the seats. He jumped a bit, startled to see anyone except the manager. He then called out saying, "Sir, I'm sorry but we're closed." The man at the bar ignored him and didn't react at all.

Miguel called out to the manager, but he must not have heard. After a few min- utes of staring, Miguel decided the guy must be drunk. He had stumbled in there somehow. Miguel approached the man, thinking he would help him call a cab. When he was standing a good foot away, he said in a loud voice, "Sir, can I help you get a ride home?" The man said nothing. Miguel inched closer and repeated, "Sir…" Just then, the man fell over onto the floor and began writhing.

Startled, Miguel took a few steps back. Then, the man flipped over onto his stomach and slid his body across the ground with his forearms, moving quickly toward Miguel who stumbled backward to avoid him. The man was making ter- rible grunting noises as he slithered closer and then grabbed Miguel's leg. Miguel screamed out when, finally, the manager burst through the door. Miguel looked anxiously at the manager and yelled, "Help me!" But when he looked back, the man had disappeared. Miguel was alone on the ground, and the manager was extremely confused.

Miguel tried to explain it to his boss, but he just brushed it off and said Miguel's mind had played tricks on him, that he was just working too hard.

The National Theater

"Though this be madness, yet there is method in't."

Those famous lines from Shakespeare's Hamlet were spoken under ghastly circumstances on the stage of the National Theatre in 1885. John McCullough was a promising actor in the title role. It was the last part he would play because later he was brutally murdered by a fellow actor. This actor hated him because a beautiful actress was attracted to McCullough.

Today this doomed actor remains a part of the theater both in body and spirit. Not only was he buried in a cellar under the stage, but his spirit continues to haunt the premises long after he "shuffled off this mortal coil."

The National Theatre.

Every actor at the National Theatre finds it more difficult than usual to con- centrate on their performances because they can't help feeling they are being watched. The ghost of John McCullough studies any young actor who attempts the same roles that he performed.

John is a jealous spirit who feels a sense of unfinished business. Today this ghost is sure that it should have been him that earned the latest standing ovation. And he should have received that latest glowing write-up in the newspaper. McCullough has shown up backstage, checking on props and stage mechanisms.

119

Actors have reported props and costume pieces disappearing, the likely culprit being this ghost who believed they were rightfully his. Most unnerving of all, his spirit will appear during live shows and dressed in full costume, such as the Roman centurion Virginius, the ruthless general Macbeth, and the vengeful Hamlet - all the characters driven mad in some way.

The John Wilson Building

The John A. Wilson Building houses the office of the Mayor of Washington, D.C.. After opening in 1908, the building was named simply the District Building, but in 1994 it was renamed in honor of the City Council member and civil rights activist, John A. Wilson, who committed suicide the year before while serving as Chair of the Council.

Despite the tragic circumstances of Wilson's death, there have been no sightings of his spirit around the building. Instead, something more grim and further in the past haunts this site. Before this building was constructed, there was a streetcar power station.

By the late nineteenth century, D.C. had a public streetcar system that used horses to pull the cars. After an outbreak of the flu among the horses that crippled the city's transit system, officials looked for an alternative. A few decades later, they got funding to embed cables in the ground to pull the cars around the city. To do this they built a large coal power station at the John Wilson location to run the city's entire streetcar system. The new system opened early in 1897 and was going well until tragedy struck. In September 1897, a fire broke out at the station and two workers were trapped in the building and were burned alive. Members of the fire brigade reported hearing their screams as they put out the raging fire.

Years later one custodian told a story about hearing someone calling out early one morning. He followed the sound to what he thought was its source. He yelled through the door, "Are you okay, do you need help?" The person just kept saying, "It's too hot, I can't get around it. Please help me!" The custodian usually had a master key, but he had lent it to one of the younger workers. He yelled the worker's name, but they weren't around. Then he started bashing the door, hoping to break it in. "Help me, please, it's burn-ing, my skin is burn- ing!" the voice screamed. Finally, he cracked the hinge on the door and burst through, but the room was empty, and the voice was gone. He swears to this day that he heard something and that it wasn't just his mind playing tricks. And as more people claim to hear screams or feel intense heat when nothing is around, the more likely his story seems.

As a side note: Because of the new cable system, the city also hired "pitmen" who sat in alcoves under the street and attached electrical plows to the underside of cars as they barreled on by. Several men were electrocuted, and at least three died after poking their heads out of their hole a little too far when a streetcar passed by.

The Willard Hotel

The Willard InterContinental Hotel was built in 1847 by combining stores, restaurants, and other establishments together into one unified hotel, and this accounts for its unorthodox shape.

Many famous individuals have frequented this hotel, from Presidents to literary figures. Abraham Lincoln came often. Famous nineteenth Century poet Emily Dickinson stayed here,along with Mark Twain and Charles Dick- ens. Even the great magician Harry Houdini came to the Willard. When Presi- dent Warren Harding died, his successor Calvin Coolidge made it the temporary White House while he waited for Harding's widow to move out of the White House.

But the spectral figure that is seen lounging in the hotel lobby is the ghost of Civil War general and former President Ulysses S. Grant. When Grant was inaugurated, he had a great deal of experience commanding an army, but the task of running the Executive Branch was overwhelming. The best part of his day was when he strolled to the Willard to sit in his favorite chair in the lobby, smoking one of his famous cigars and sipping brandy to get a few minutes of peace.

Unfortunately for President Grant, the peace was usually short-lived. His lei- surely trips to the Willard became well known which meant that business and civic leaders would track him down and surround him to influence public policy. Instead of enjoying a few moments of relaxation, Grant found himself fending off political vultures that he called "lobbyists."

Countless guests and staff members over the years claim to have seen him sitting in that same favorite chair and enjoying his brandy. Others have been confused   by the pungent scent of cigar smoke filling the lobby, because smoking has been banned.

The Willard Hotel.

ADDITIONAL SCARES

Voice App. Ghost Stories

JUST ASK
alexa

works with the
Google Assistant

Listen to one of over 200 narrated ghost
stories from home on Alexa or Google Assistant
Alexa: "Alexa, Open Ghost Adventures"
Google Home: "Hey Google, Talk to Ghost Adventures"

US GH∶ST
ADVENTURES

Who Doesn't Want To Hear a Ghost Story on Echo? ★★★★★

I love the idea of listening to a spooky story at night. The stories are all very interesting and entertaining and have
been pulled from many different cities across the U.S. I would listen to them in a distraction free place so as that I
can listen attentively. It's a great way to learn about US history in an engaging way. I highly recommend trying this
skill, especially with a group. It is easily one of my top favorite Alexa skills for sure!

Sana - Amazon Prime Review

Turn Your **Phone** Into A Ghost Tour!

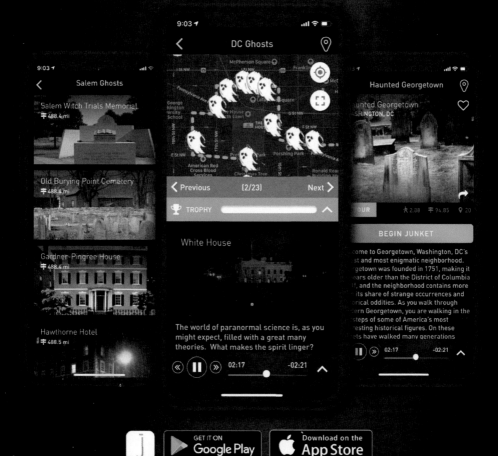

Download the Junket app for GPS-based, audio guided Ghost Tours of over 25 cities across the U.S. Hear terrifying stories and see historical haunted places as the app delivers ghost tours at your fingertips! Take a tour in person on location, or from home!

Visit usghostadventures.com/ghost-tour-app

Aqueduct Bridge, circa 1900.

CHAPTER III - PART 2

Haunted Georgetown

Georgetown, is Washington, D.C.'s oldest neighborhood. Georgetown was founded in 1751, 40 years before the District of Columbia. Georgetown's distinct character reflects its original purpose as a portage and commercial hub on the Potomac River.

Despite its humble beginnings, Georgetown has seen dozens of this country's greatest leaders walk its streets. Many of them studied at Georgetown University on the high bluff overlooking much of Washington, D.C.

Georgetown has had the political character of the lesser sibling all its life. Perhaps this is why it was a hotbed of Confederate spying, during the Civil War. This sympathy with the 'other,' has been absorbed into its character, adopting contrarian views often for the sake of difference alone. Yet it provided patriots, too. Georgetown sent Thomas Lynch, Sr. and Thomas Lynch, Jr. to the Conti- nental Congress where the younger Lynch was a signer of the Declaration of Independence. The British held Georgetown in an iron grip of occupation during the war.

During the Civil War, Georgetown and Washington, D.C. were close enough to the theatres of battle that several buildings were commandeered as hospitals. Little Women author Louisa May Alcott served as a nurse in one Georgetown hospi- tal, describing the seemingly endless stream of brutalized casualties pulled by exhausted horses. So many of these men drew their final breath here in George- town, and so many of the continue to haunt the town today.

Aside from the Civil War, the town has a rich history of hauntings and ghosts, separate and distinct from its glamorous neighbor. More real, more accessible, and more human. But the lives that ended here are no less tragic, less worthy of our thought, or less likely to produce a ghostly echo down the years.

Home of Dr. Grafton Tyler

Dr. Tyler was a Southern sympathizer who lived in this home in the 1860s. It is said that he closed his shutters every day during the Civil War, even in sweltering heat. He couldn't bear the sight of the U.S. flag that flew over the Ladies' Seminary across the street.

Dr. Tyler's cousin was the Confederate General Robert E. Lee and his brother- in-law, Walter Bowie, was a southern spy. At the height of the war, Bowie was locked up in the Capitol Prison where he was to be executed for the crime of espionage. Mrs. Tyler, who was Bowie's sister and also a spy, visited her brother. When she kissed him goodbye, she passed a note from her mouth to his.

The note said she had bribed a guard to abandon his post for the night. Bowie then was able to escape and flee to the South.

Home of Dr. Grafton Tyler. Photo Credit: Chayna Sellers.

At the end of the war when Richmond was captured, Dr. Tyler's house was the only home with darkened windows on the street. Noticing this, Union soldiers gathered around his front steps and serenaded the doctor with songs of celebra- tion and hung the Union's colors on his door.

M Street Bridge

In 1788, a wooden draw bridge was built over Rock Creek connecting George- town with the newly developing area to the east, the site of the nation's capital. People needed a level crossing over Rock Creek's steep ravine to reach the pastureland in the area that is now downtown Washington, D.C.. However, the newly constructed bridge carried too much traffic and it collapsed soon after it was built. Passengers in a stagecoach were killed when the coach fell down into the ravine.

When another bridge was built in the early 1800s, Georgetown residents reported seeing a lone stagecoach on moonless nights racing eastward down what is now M Street and then suddenly vanishing. Other witnesses reported seeing the apparition of a drummer boy, which has been linked to legends of a young military drummer who was knocked off the bridge and fell to his death in a freak windstorm. In the quiet hours before dawn, witnesses said they heard the faint sound of drumming, growing louder and still louder near the center of the bridge, and then becoming quiet as they approached. And one more spirit has haunted this bridge, as well. Witnesses have encountered a headless man, seen from the east side of the bridge, whose story remains a mystery.

M Street Bridge - M Street east of 28th Street. Photo Credit: Chayna Sellers.

Site of the Union Hotel and Tavern

M Street at the corner of 30th Street is the heart of Georgetown's more than two-century-old commercial district. On the northeast corner, where a single- story brick building, housing a bank, now stands, was once the site of the old Union Hotel and Tavern building, which was considered one of the finest hotels. The Union Hotel was built in 1796 when Georgetown had become part of the District of Columbia. At various times it hosted George Washington, Francis Scott Key, Napoleon III, Robert Fulton and Washington Irving. When the Federal Government officially moved to D.C. in 1800, President John Adams stayed at the hotel while construction was being completed on the White House.

During the Civil War, the Union Hotel was commandeered by the government to be used as a hospital. Throughout the war, the capitol city was close enough to the front that its hospital beds were filled. By the end of the war, more than eighteen thousand soldiers had died in D.C.'s hospitals. While working there as a nurse, Little Women author Louisa May Alcott wrote: "Long trains of army wagons kept up a perpetual rumble from morning until night. Ambulances rattled to and fro with busy surgeons, nurses taking an airing or convalescents going in parties to be fitted for artificial limbs. Strings of sorry looking horses passed, saying as plainly as dumb creatures could, 'why in a city full of them is there no hospital for us?' Often a cart came by, with several rough coffins in it and no mourners following; barouches, with invalid officers, rolled around the corner and carriage loads of pretty children, with black coachmen, footmen and maids."

Site of the Union Hotel and Tavern – 30th & M Street, (now Sun Trust Bank). Photo Credit: Chayna Sellers.

The Old Stone House

On M Street between 30th and 31st Streets, the north side of M Street's retail store- fronts give way to a scene of Georgetown as it existed nearly 250 years ago.

The Old Stone House is Washington, D.C.'s oldest building. Built in 1765 by Christopher and Rachel Layman, it was sold soon after completion to Cassandra Chew, a wealthy Georgetown widow. She expanded the original structure over the decades. It was a private home for nearly two hundred years and many ghosts became associated with it, including:

-- a woman wearing a brown dress standing near the mantelpiece
-- a large woman standing sometimes on the stairs and other times in the kitchen
-- a blond man in a blue jacket
-- a man wearing short pants and stockings
-- a woman rocking in a chair on the third floor
-- a small boy running in the third floor hallway
-- a man in colonial-era clothing in the upstairs bedroom
-- a young girl with curly hair running up and down the staircase
-- an African American boy

But the most malevolent spirit has been nicknamed "George." According to reports, George has choked and pushed visitors and has caused a sudden cold- ness and a sense of overwhelming dread.

The Old Stone House - 3051 M Street NW. Photo Credit: Chayna Sellers.

Chesapeake & Ohio (C&O) Canal

In the eighteenth and nineteenth centuries, Georgetown was settled as the last port town that was accessible to boats going up the Potomac River. The C&O Canal was built during the 1850s to allow river traffic to move past Great Falls. During the Civil War, the canal was used as a bathing area by the fifteen thousand Union troops quartered in this neighborhood. The Evening Star complained about the lack of morals exhibited by the troops and wrote, "Is it proper for the 1st Massachusetts to bathe in the canal at all hours? What aggravates the matter is that the bathers range themselves along the towpath in the costume of the Greek slave, minus the chain and in attitudes anything but peaceful or becoming."

According to D.C. historian Tim Krepp, the C&O Canal has had a haunted reputation since its heyday in the 1890s. A police officer who was walking one of the city's most dangerous beats along the canal one dark night, came upon a ghostly apparition under a bridge. The figure was a man holding an old-fashioned barber's straight razor and both the man and the razor were dripping with blood. The officer reported the sighting immediately. And later that same night, a local landlord attempted to murder a boarder in his boardinghouse. His weap- on was a barber's straight razor. Ever since, the police, in Washington's seventh precinct, call this the "Dead Man's Beat."

Chesapeake & Ohio (C&O) Canal. Photo Credit: Chayna Sellers.

The Georgetown Bluffs

In the summer of 1755 during the French and Indian war, British General Edward Braddock set out on a disastrous military expedition. Braddock wanted to capture the French Fort Duquesne. On the way he became engaged in the Battle of Monongahela, near what is now Braddock, Pennsylvania. The British force of thirteen hundred regular soldiers and colonial fighting men was ambushed by the enemy, and nine hundred soldiers were killed or wounded. General Braddock was killed but one of the survivors was a young Virginia volunteer named George Washington.

Reports of ghostly hauntings by General Braddock and his men go back before the Civil War and include witness hearing loud military orders, hooves on the roads, and marching soldiers on the anniversary of the departure of General Braddock's expedition from Georgetown.

A Spooky Georgian house, high in the Georgetown Bluffs. Photo Credit: Chayna Sellers.

Prospect Cottage

The "exorcist stairs" area set of steep, stone stairs made famous by an appearance in the climactic scene of the 1973 film, The Exorcist, based on the novel by Georgetown graduate William Peter Blatty. At the top of these stairs stands a house on the site of Prospect Cottage, a very old structure which was known for being haunted during the nineteenth century.

It was the home of Mrs. E. D. E. N. Southworth, a mother of two who was beaten and then abandoned by her husband in the 1850s, and who then took to writing novels in order to support her children. When the Confederates beat back Union soldiers at the Battle of Manassas, many believed Georgetown would be attacked and ransacked by Confederate soldiers. Mrs. Southworth barricaded herself and her children in her cottage, and prayed, "There's only three of us here. How will we survive if the Confederates come?" According to Mrs. Southworth, a faint voice responded, "There are four of you here, and you'll be fine." She and her children survived the war and then lived in the cottage for years afterward. Subsequent owners of the cottage reported seeing the figure of Mrs. Southworth in the room that had been her library. When the last of the books were removed from that room, the reports of the apparition ceased as well.

Prospect Cottage - 3600 Prospect Street NW - "The Exorcist stairs". Photo Credit: Chayna Sellers.

Halcyon House

This 30,000 square-foot mansion was built by Benjamin Stoddert in 1787. Stoddert was the nation's first Secretary of the Navy. Later the house was said to be a safe house on the Underground Railroad for runaway slaves. In 1900, Albert Clemens, a nephew of Mark Twain, bought this house and began the process of adding alterations that would last the rest of his life.

Clemens believed that continuing to renovate the structure would extend his life. He died in 1938, leaving a larger house, but it was also full of bizarre rooms which had no entrance and hallways leading nowhere. There is even a crypt located beneath the basement. Halcyon House is said to be haunted by runaway
slaves who were apprehended and then tortured and killed. Their voices have been heard in the basement begging for mercy. There are also reports of Benjamin Stoddert walking the halls, siting in the oldest parts of the house, and whisper- ing. Another spirit, a woman, has been seen by passers-by standing in an upstairs window. And guests at Halcyon House have been disturbed in the night by poltergeists on beds spinning their bodies around separate from their heads. A six-year-old boy reported the figure of a wom-an waking him and moving his bed covers.

Halcyon House - 3400 Prospect Street NW. Photo Credit: Chayna Sellers.

facebook.com/usghostadventures
usghostadv
usgadventures
usghostadvntrs
pinterest.com/usghostadventures
usghostadventures
#usghostadventures

Afterword

May we reject a fear of the unknown and embrace the spirit of curiosity to pursue the unexplained. Today's science may not give us the answers we seek to reveal the unknown frontiers, but one day it will. While one may not believe in "ghosts" in the traditional sense, we can agree that there is much in our universe that remains unexplained. It's been less than 500 years since we accepted that the Earth was round, and that nothing revolves around it. It's been less than 100 years since humanity split the atom. People continue to make new discoveries every year, and we hope that one day science can explain what we call ghosts.

Until then, we aim to make sense of these unexplained events and uncover the stories behind them. Only a small amount of encounters have been captured here, and in the pages of the accompanying volumes. If these tales have interested you, and awakened a curiosity, you have found your tribe in US Ghost Adventures. Across America, groups of people gather to hear our tales of the hauntings and history of spirits of the past. We welcome you to join any of our experiences to hear the stories and see the places where these events took place, whether that is in person, or watching from home on GhostFlix.

With respect and reverence, we humbly seek to honor the memory of those who have passed, celebrate their lives, learn from their wisdom, and seek to live better lives through their lessons.

Respectfully,

Lance Zaal, Founder
US Ghost Adventures
usghostadventures.com